Gifts for the Living

Conversations with Caregivers on Death and Dying

BettyClare Moffatt, M.A.

Sponsored by
Progressive Nursing Services

IBS Press
Santa Monica, California

ISBN# 0-9616605-3-8

Library of Congress Card Catalog Number Pending

First Printing, 1988
Published by IBS Press
744 Pier Ave.
Santa Monica, CA 90405

Dedication

For Joey Shea, who,
when confronted with Death, cried,
"Wow! Death is a great adventure. I can hardly wait."

Acknowledgements

With grateful acknowledgement to the following contributors:

Stuart Altschuler, M.S., M.F.C.C., Executive Director, Los Angeles Center For Living

Chelsea Psychotherapy Associates:
Dixie Beckham, C.S.W, A.C.S.W.
Luis Palacios-Jimenez, C.S.W., A.C.S.W.
Vincent John Patti, C.S.W.
Michael Shernoff, C.S.W., A.C.S.W.

Cassandra Christenson, R.N.
Director of Education, Los Angeles Center For Living
Author, *A Guidance Through Death*

Helen Thomas Cook

Jim Geary
Executive Director, Shanti Project, San Francisco

Bill Hodgson, R.N.
AIDS Home Health Specialist

David Kessler, R.N.
President, Progressive Nursing Services

Reverend Margie Ann Nicola
Assistant Minister, Unity-By-The-Sea

Reverend Carol W. Parrish-Harra
Minister, Light of Christ Community Church
Author, *A New Age Handbook On Death And Dying*

Bobby Reynolds

Deborah Roth, C.S.W.
The Center For Help In Time Of Loss
Author, *Stepping Stones To Grief Recovery*

Joey Shea

Micael Tapia

Reverend John-Alexis Viereck
Minister, St. Augustine-By-The-Sea Episcopal Church
Founder, Chapel Of St. John

Laurie Williams, R.N.

Marianne Williamson
Spiritual Teacher, *A Course In Miracles*
Founder, Los Angeles Center For Living

And Special Thanks To Progressive Nursing Services

Contents

Foreword

Death is a mystery to most people. Until we confront it in our immediate family, it's something we read about in the papers, it's something that happens to other people. We can feel great compassion and sympathy for others who are experiencing it and at the same time have no concept of what "it" is. Although it's something that one day happens to everyone, most of us feel it is so far down the road in life that any thought of it is submerged. Because of our denial that death occurs to the young and the old, the well and the sick, the rich and the poor, we are uneducated and unprepared when our first confrontation with physical mortality occurs. That certainly was my experience.

My father was killed in an automobile accident when I was fifteen years old. Living in the Midwest, my mother and I followed the traditional funeral arrangements. For three days we sat from early morning until late night in the funeral home "receiving visitors." It was a dance that had to be danced no matter what the price. We were so caught up in other people's reactions that our own feelings were put aside. We simply existed in a vacuum, maintaining the semblance of what was expected. My mother was placed in a doctor's care whose answer for her pain was sleeping pills. When we would finally go home at night, she would fall into bed and I was left to survive as best I could. Somehow I was lost in the shuffle. No one's fault, just the way it was. Understandable but regrettable.

I can remember standing at the screen door of the funeral home the second evening, looking out and wondering what I was supposed to do. I didn't know what a person did when they "grieved" for their father.

I didn't particularly feel anything except isolation, confusion, and fear. This thing that laid in the casket wasn't my father. My dad was a volatile personality that was either laughing, angry, or intensely involved in something. I had been told he had been badly mangled in the accident and yet the face and body showed no signs of injury. Maybe they were wrong. Maybe my dad wasn't dead, whatever that was.

The nightmare of the wake finally came to an end, the people went home and back to their lives and mother and I returned to an empty house, an empty life. I remember some friends of mine came by the house and asked if I wanted to go for a coke, and I didn't know whether to go or not. Should I leave my mother? Was it proper? Was I supposed to look sad? I still felt numb.

Because there was no one to guide me through my grief, I stayed in the "loss" mode for years and years. My behavior patterns were affected and I formed belief systems based on the fear of something I didn't understand. The fear of rejection and abandonment was paramount in all of my relationships. I very effectively became a rejecter because I knew how to deal with *that* mode of action, whereas I still didn't understand, or know how to cope with, rejection and loss.

I am convinced that because "death and dying" was *unknown* and feared, and because I was not encouraged to embrace and explore this unknown, I lived my life in fear of *anything* that was *unknown*.

In the ministry, one of the most challenging services I had to learn was ministering to the dying and to the family unit "left behind." My observations have reinforced my earlier experience. People simply are not prepared for death. Not the person making the transition nor the family support group. Dying, death, and grieving are experiences that should not be shunted under the table nor should it be taken for granted that everyone knows how to die and to grieve. Both are shrouded in mystery and certainly not something discussed in our culture. Perhaps this book will begin to change that.

It has been my observation that most of those who are dying desperately need someone who isn't afraid of them and their situation. And many times they need to talk about their condition and their death. Unfortunately, sometimes the family and friends simply cannot fill this need. Perhaps they are in denial and will not face the process. Perhaps it reminds them of their own mortality. Perhaps it represents too much of a loss for them to acknowledge. As a counselor, much of my service is simply listening and loving. When people ask for advice, I encourage them to consider alternative ways of thinking and feeling. I remind them consistently that they are loved, that they are important, and that God loves them, because often the dying feel as though they are being punished by God for some known or unknown deed or thought.

When the illness is a long and slow deterioration, some come to a space and time when they make their peace with the process, life, and their God. Usually when peace is experienced, death follows soon. Others put up a valiant struggle to the last breath. Others seem to be waiting for permission from the family.

Those that are diagnosed as "terminally ill" are sometimes left to face their death alone. Many times the family and friends will fall by the wayside as the condition worsens and the time drags on, leaving the patient with a sense of alienation and isolation to struggle alone with their death and pain. It seems to me that the family and friends cannot deal with their loved one's drama for it becomes *their* drama. They simply cannot handle the emotions involved and so they avoid the whole situation. Understandable but regrettable.

Fortunately, I have aligned with a philosophy and belief system that has taught me life and death are one and the same and God is equally invested in both. As I have made my peace with my reality I can now allow my loved ones to make their choices, to live their lives as they need to and then to leave this plane of existence and enter another. I can afford to let them go, even though I experience "loss" and grieve for my loss, knowing that I will pass through the pain. Because of my spiritual life I know that my loved ones are loved and received in love as they experience all dimensions of life.

Death is not an ending, it is a beginning — for the deceased and the survivor. Death is but the closing of one door and the opening of another in the adventure of living. The pain that is experienced is the result of clinging to one form of expression while entering another. For the deceased *and* the survivor, the pain is part of resisting change. I have seen lovers reunited at the last breath, I have seen spiritual understanding expand at the last breath, I have seen broken families restored, I have seen such great beauty and infinite peace expressed with the last breath. I don't believe it is our fear of death that is the great challenge to us, but our fear of life. If we each understood the secrets of life we would not fear death.

REVEREND MARGIE ANN NICOLA
Assistant Minister, Unity-By-The-Sea
May, 1988

Introduction

My son Michael died of AIDS July 14, 1986. He was twenty-eight years old. Out of that experience has come an intense desire not only to serve in some capacity but also to understand. To understand and to heal.

In our Western culture, we are taught from early childhood to be afraid of death. We are shielded from the mystery. We are shielded from our fears.

Courageous, loving serviceful men and women step forth to care for the terminally ill patient, whether it is a child dying of Leukemia, a young man dying of AIDS, or an old man dying of cancer. Doctors, nurses, hospice attendants, clergy, social workers, therapists, family members; all of us are drawn into the circle of the dying at some point in our lives. And most of us recoil from the experience, at least initially, because we don't know what to do. We are given platitudes about how it's supposed to be. We are told of the great light and joy beyond death, but who teaches us about the before and the during?

For while death can be a kind friend, the dying process itself can be agonizing, not only for the dying person struggling to let go, but for his loved ones watching, waiting, hoping. . .for what? A miracle of resurrection? We can hold the person back or we can release them in unconditional love and acceptance, but *how* do we do that? *How* do we deal with our own feelings as we watch a loved one suffer? How do we deal with our own recovery period, when mourning in our culture is often seen as a brisk "Now, now, stiff upper lip. Just get on with your own life now." When it is seen as almost indecent for the survivors to fall apart. Our loneliness, our deep hurting, must often be done alone, out of sight of family and friends. We must "get over it." We must pick up the pieces and go on. We must not burden others with our grief. We are taught to be stoics. And when the dam breaks, as it will, oh it will, and the sorrow and the rage break forth, our feelings often scare us as much as they scare others.

Well-meaning people around us, even professional helpers, sometimes use platitudes to hide their own bewilderment and uncomfortableness with death. When my grandson Zachary died at the age of eighteen months, well-meaning family members told my son and daughter-in-law "There, there it's all right. After all you have another son." As if each *life*, each child, were not as precious as the other, as if each loss were not as valid as the next.

In this age of AIDS, we are forced to confront our bewilderment with the dying process on a grand scale. We wanted so for my son, Michael to be healed. Then, as the body and mind deteriorated, we wanted so for his poor body to be at peace, and his soul to be happy, at home in God. And yet we hurt. Oh how we hurt! Out of that hurt has grown a determination to share with others what I have learned about death. To share what I have learned about love, about courage, and about the transformation of the human spirit.

Those of us who choose to work in caregiving ways with the dying and with the survivors are confronting our own pain and bewilderment daily. We are transforming our own fears into what I like to call "serviceful joy." And because of the sometimes daily confrontation with the mystery, we are, in brief, rare, intense moments, in communion with spirit, whether we would call it God, Jesus Christ, a Higher Power or simply the Holy Spirit. The intensity of our confrontation with Spirit can burn us out, and/or it can transform our lives. For we are never the same again after the confrontation, after the pass through to the mystery of death, whether it is a near-death experience or holding the hand of a dying patient and "midwifing" them through the next step. However we help, there is a place beyond that we *too* can glimpse and can be a part of — a Holy Instant of communion. Fear is then transformed to love and all the "me-ness" of flesh and bone and chaotic emotions can fall away, if only for an instant, as we reach out, one hand to another, one heart to another.

And then we receive. In the midst of it all we receive the Gifts For the Living. These gifts are myriad; they are as individual and special as each human life. Yet I have found while interviewing so many professional caregivers that there are certain Gifts For the Living that are constant. When we can find and recognize and experience each of these gifts, we are healed. Our emptiness can be refilled and we *can* continue — at a level of intensity and integrity previously undreamed of by our small, ego-filled selves. These are the gifts:

The Gift of Adventure

The Gift of the Generations

The Gift of Honesty

The Gift of Healing

The Gift of Understanding

The Gift of Guidance

The Gift of Caring

The Gift of Unconditional Love

The Gift of Transformation

For every caregiver that reaches out to someone before, during, and after this mystery called death, these Gifts For the Living are offered. Many are overlapping gifts. Life, like death, is often untidy; uncontainable in neat sentences that wrap an emotion into crystallized thought. The Gifts For the Living follow no dogma, no one set of religious beliefs, although I am indeed blessed to have chapters by clergy. These gifts are not even neat psychological techniques. Caregiver therapists, like caregiver doctors, nurses, mothers, struggle themselves to find meaning in their work. What I do offer here is a series of extraordinary conversations with professional caregivers who work in some way with death and dying and who, with clarity and compassion, offer their own insights into the dying process and how working with the terminally ill has changed their lives.

As I spoke with caregivers, certain themes emerged again and again:

That we are afraid sometimes that we will "catch death" if we are around it.

That doctors and nurses and professional caregivers are taught detachment, and that detachment can be a barrier, an armored defense against feeling and caring.

That caregivers often make jokes to cover their own fear and pain.

That survivors are often brushed aside or uncomfortably reassured by caregivers who are themselves afraid of death.

That nursing schools don't teach you how to handle death and dying or the concerns of the family.

That death is often categorized as "a good death" or "an awful death," — societal judgments which perpetuate themselves.

That not mentioning death does not mean it isn't there or it will go away.

That we are taught to worship youth and strong, beautiful bodies, and so we save bodies at all costs, hooking them up to every possible machine until the life has gone out of the soul and the personality, and only a shell of the former self remains.

That one death experience can trigger other unresolved feelings of loss to be worked through.

That death is the last taboo. We now can talk openly about sexuality, but not about death.

That people who work in death and dying fields often feel as though they are in a "war zone," and others out there are "civilians" who don't understand.

That in spite of increased life-spans we are *all* going to have to be faced with our own death and the deaths of others.

That the horror can often outweigh the peace and acceptance.

That we are neither ghoulish or sick ourselves if we work with dying people, neither are we noble saints like Mother Theresa. We are just reaching out to do our part.

That we don't have to know everything about life and death, but our efforts to understand can make it bearable and can help us to live more peacefully in the world of the flesh and the spirit.

That we must continue to give to ourselves in order to avoid not only burnout and callousness, but exhaustion and sickness ourselves. We don't have to be martyrs on a "suicide mission" in order to serve.

That it *is* often overwhelming and that when we take care of a dying patient, there is no "reward" in the form of restored health — the end result is death.

That we must continually recharge *self* and nurture *self* because life does indeed go on even as death goes on.

That it's all right to take a vacation, a sabbatical, a breather. The work is still there whenever we are ready to return to it.

That comfort is sometimes the only thing we can give, and it is enough.

That we don't have to or need to argue with others over what we do or don't do. Acceptance of our own feelings helps us to be more compassionate and courageous.

That we must love ourselves as we love others in order to be equal to the task.

Joey Shea, an eighty-three year old man dying of cancer, summed it up best when I interviewed him five days before he died.

"I've done it all, I've seen it all," he cried. "You tell them all out there what I said. I have looked death in the face and I say, "Wow! Death is a great adventure. I can hardly wait."

For Joey and for Michael and for David and Laurie and Cassandra and Stewart and Margie Ann and Jim and Bobby and Bill and Marianne and for my mother and for all who contributed so lovingly and willingly to this book, and for those of you who may be confronting death for the first time, and especially to Progressive Nursing Services, whose 200 plus caregivers go out daily to meet Joey Shea's "great adventure" with death, I offer these Gifts For the Living.

BETTYCLARE MOFFATT
May, 1988

The Gift
of
Adventure

COME HOME

Come home.
The tower waits.
The sea is still.
Dark gone. Light breaks.
Do what you will.

Serene, the tower.
Serene, the waiting sea.
Come home
Alone
Wherever you may be.

The hour creates the hour
I come to tell you.
Only
Come home
To filling sea,
To towers that will not fall
To infinity.
I come to tell you of that energy.

And of that high and holy power
within
Your own serene and inner citadel.
Come home.

— BETTYCLARE MOFFATT

1

Joey Shea is a remarkable man. I met him when his son, David Kessler, asked me to interview him for this book. When I came into his son's home, where he lived for the last few weeks of his life, I saw a hospital bed drawn up to glass doors that led into a patio garden. The room was full of sunshine and light, and I could hardly believe that the vital man sitting up in bed was actually diagnosed as having only a few days more to live. Joey dominated the room as he dominated the conversation. This, despite tubes in his nose and an IV attached to his arm. His eighty-three year old girlfriend Mabel was there, as well as Laurie, his nurse. David, his son, sat on the side of Joey's bed as we talked, and paused often to embrace his father. At one point we watched one of Joey's videotapes of him performing for a nursing home, singing, dancing, clowning. He was obviously proud of what he had accomplished in his life.

Before we started the interview, David and I talked at great length about his father. With remarkable clarity and honesty he told of his relationship with his father and his own feelings about death, both as an only son losing the one closest to him, and as a professional caregiver working with the terminally ill.

DK: The thing about my father that's very interesting is that my father is eighty-three, he was in show business and started out with Milton Berle and Danny Thomas and all of them, and he achieved medium fame, never quite made it to the big time. And that's something that obviously he's hung onto all these years. And he's always been an entertainer all these years. I mean even up until two months ago he was singing in old folk's homes, to entertain them. And just enjoying it and loving it. But the thing is that last night we were talking and he has so much invested in that part of his past, so much of his identity, that when I was talking about you coming, he was saying to me, "Well does she know that I used to entertain?" And I said, "Now you need to know that she's coming here to talk to you about death because you're so open about it and the thing that's so important that I would love for you to understand is that who you *were* was wonderful and that was a great gift you gave entertainment, but she doesn't know a thing about that and she's coming because of who you are *today*. And who you are *today* is just as special and just as important as that person was."

BCM: *That's beautiful.*

DK: I want him to realize that right now the gift he can give people in talking openly about death will be as powerful as any gift he ever gave in the thirties or forties.

BCM: *You're right.*

DK: That he will touch as many lives and give as much happiness. And that it really is *this moment* that's important. You know in a way I think it was nice for him to hear that. Because I think it's probably been a long time since he's felt important about something.

BCM: *It's nice for people to feel important instead of being in isolation. They need to feel just as valued and loved as always during this intense ultimate experience that they're going through.*

DK: Right. Absolutely.

BCM: *Well, how are you able to be so open with Joe?*

DK: Well, I tell you, I'm someone who believes in total honesty. And one of the things we have at Progressive Nursing Services is the dying patient's Bill of Rights and a person has a right to honesty, no matter what's going on in their life. And I feel like the only way that I've gotten my relationships in my life to work is with total honesty. And there have been times that I've thought, "I shouldn't be just sitting at his bedside, I should be taking care of him, I should be strong." And then I thought, "No, whatever I'm feeling is exactly what I should be feeling." So I show my feelings in front of him. If I'm angry I express it, and if I'm joyful, I express that too. I tell him that I'm sad about this, but it's fine, it's okay. Just approach it honestly and once you get past that, then it's amazing, you can get to the growth part of it all.

BCM: *Right. In the midst of dealing with your own feelings and with your father in this last experience, now that you're on the other side, now that you are the family member going through it, do you think that will help you in the future when you're dealing with dying patients and their families as a nurse?*

DK: Absolutely. Absolutely. There were some experiences in the hospital where his rights really got violated and I was amazed to see the medical system work so well without the patient, or without anyone asking the patient. Because people were making decisions about my father's life without talking to my father. And you know when the doctor finally said to me, "Well, we think he has cancer, we don't know if we're going to tell him, and we *haven't* told him," I said, "My father's a grown man, he's eighty-three years old, and it's my father's life, and if he has cancer he has as much right to know, if not more, than you do. And you need to go in there and talk to him about it."

BCM: *Yes. Did you always have a good relationship with your father or has that developed in maturity?*

DK: Well, it's interesting. I would say that we had a very distant relationship when I was growing up until my mother died at thirteen, at which point he and I were kind of left alone together and through that tragedy we became very close and have been close ever since. You know the interesting thing, the background of what's going on now is that my father has been so active and healthy until recently. One month ago he was walking two miles a day, he would do shows, he would love to go to Vegas and see shows and gamble and just have a good time. But then he called me up in December and said, "I have to see you right away." And I said, "What's wrong?" And he said, "Well, let me just come down and see you. And I said, "Sure, but I mean I'm worried, tell me." So then he said, "Well, I dreamed last night that I was about to die. I saw it all and it was all real clear and I feel like it's really true. I don't want this to be a tragedy. I feel it's my time and I just want to come down and let's play."

BCM: *Wow!*

DK: This was in December. He flew down here and after about four days here we went to Vegas and spent five days and just had a great time together. And we talked about it all. I thought well, who knows if it's real or not, but you never know and it's just amazing that it turns out it looks like it *is* true. He is going to die.

BCM: *What did you feel when he told you that? After he told you the dream?*

DK: Well my reaction was the same feeling he had. Let's get together immediately. And how precious time is. And we do take each other for granted so easily in this world and often don't spend the time together with the people that we love. So immediately I thought, "My God, let's get together right away just in case it is true." And, you know, with my father, he's just such a foundation of my life that there's an assumption that he's just always going to be there. I'm always going to be able to pick up the phone and he'll be there. And for it to hit me like that square in the eyes that it might not always be that way, the reality was heartbreaking.

BCM: *I have heard that when your mother or father dies that there is no one between you and eternity or there is no one between you and God, there's no one between you and the rest of your life. You are the adult with no buffer.*

DK: That's exactly what one of my first feelings was. I thought, "My mother's gone and when my father goes I'll truly be alone in the world and on my own." And it was such a scary feeling because...

BCM: *How old are you if you don't mind me asking?*

DK: I'm twenty-eight.

BCM: *Twenty-eight! You're very, very mature. You're a very old twenty-eight, right, David?*

DK: Well I do tend to think I'm probably an old soul.

BCM: *I think you are too.*

DK: So there is that feeling of I am the oldest in the family now, I am the adult.

BCM: *Are you the only child?*

DK: I'm his only child, yes. And since my mother died, there's been such a bond between him and me that to think that the bond will be gone physically is just devastating. And you know, there are interesting differences between his death and someone with AIDS and the first one is the one you mentioned. It's not a tragedy with him.

BCM: *That's true.*

DK: One thing we'll probably talk to you about is a night when he and I talked about death in the intensive care unit. One of the things I realized then was that here was an eighty-three year old man whose heart was going, who had cancer, whose body was really breaking down because of age. I was faced head-on with having to accept-this situation one hundred per cent. And I thought about how different it was than when someone has AIDS, because right till the end, you always think someone might run in that door with that cure. And I knew realistically that no one was going to run in that door with a cure for old age. You *know* that, like it or not, this was about to happen to him. And as much as I think it's important to always be hopeful, at eighty-three I knew this was probably his time.

BCM: *So is it easier acceptance, easier surrender?*

DK: It was for me in this case.

BCM: *Because it's like the leaves falling off the tree and this does happen to all of us as the next step in a long life well and joyfully lived.*

DK: And personally there's a naturalness that I feel to this, while I have such trouble feeling that naturalness when people die young.

BCM: *Also, don't you think when young people die, especially of AIDS, there's so much surrounding that fight, that struggle. I had the sense that the hardest thing for Michael to do, and for me, was to move to a place of surrender. You fight it and fight it and fight it until the last instant and then you have to do a 180 degree turn and accept and surrender in order for there to be that peaceful going on, going forward. And you don't have that with an eighty-three year old father.*

DK: Right. And I'll go ahead and tell you about that night because although he can talk about it too, I actually remember more than he does because he was on drugs at the time. There was this night in the intensive care unit where he had been heavily medicated. They were trying to keep him out of it, as we do sometimes in the hospitals. Let's keep the person out of their life while we work on their body. And he was having arrhythmias left and right, which means that his heart wasn't beating in rhythm. And they were giving him this and giving him that and I was sitting there and I was crying. And it was amazing to me how uncomfortable a man crying in a hospital makes people.

BCM: *Really? Even at your dying father's bedside.*

DK: Yes. Especially in intensive care. Because in intensive care they're very used to dealing with machines and valves, but they're not used to someone just sitting there. And it was amazing how I could sense their uncomfortableness about trying to console me.

BCM: *Do you think they wanted the human to be gone and let them be about their work and you not come in with all your feelings, that sort of thing?*

DK: At times, yes. Yes. You know there certainly are those people that see the family members as an interruption of their work.

BCM: *Yes, that's true.*

DK: So I did feel that way sometimes. I was sitting there crying and he was sleeping. Then he magically woke up and he said to me, "What's going on, what are you crying about?" I tried to pull myself together and I said, "Well, your heart's not doing well tonight and they asked me to stay here and they don't think you're going to make it through the night." He just sat there and he kind of looked for a minute at me, and then he said, "Well, I don't know what to say. I've had a good life, and I've had eighty-three years, and you know you talk all the time about people with AIDS. They're dying at twenty-five. I have nothing to complain about."

BCM: *Isn't that a remarkable statement from a dying man. ''I have nothing to complain about?''*

DK: Right. Exactly. Nothing to complain about at eighty-three years. Then he cried a little bit with me and we reminisced about some personal things and talked about the fact that we're not going to be here in this same world together anymore. And once again I thought how no one was going to rush in the door and save him. Because he did ask me whether there was a chance that they could save him or not. And I said, "Well, the reality is they may get you through tonight and they may help you a little longer, but it's just that age has caught up to you." And he and I had had one previous conversation when he was down here from Vegas and he reiterated what he said then, "I know this is going to be hard on you, David, but time heals." Then he said, "In a lot of ways in the past few years my life has been boring. I wake up every morning with the mind of a forty-year-old and I'm reminded that I'm an eighty-three-year-old man. I can't do the things I want to do, I can't be the person that I want to be anymore. It just feels right that it's time to move on." And finally he said to me, "In a lot of ways I'm real excited about it."

BCM: *That's wonderful.*

DK: And we probably continued on crying for about an hour and once we really got past the sadness, we started exploring. We talked about death, about the hereafter. We were saying, "Well, what do you think it's going to be like with each of us?" And you know he was talking about how much he missed my mother and the fact that he was thinking a lot about his parents. And we were just saying, "Well, do you think that all of a sudden you'll be on the other side and that it will be Mom there greeting you and your parents? Or do you think all of a sudden that you'll just be this spirit or this light and there will be another spirit or light next to you and you'll realize that this is the same feeling that you got from my mother and that it's her? Or that you'll be surrounded by a warmth all of a sudden, and you'll realize you haven't felt that particular warmth since your parents were here? What's it going to be like?" And then we talked about the possibility of what if it's reincarnation. What if you're going to wake up in this brand new body raring to go. And how exciting that will be. And we talked about all those sayings that we have, about youth is wasted on the young, and if I knew then what I know now.

BCM: *Yeah. (Laughter).*

DK: And we thought, what if you get to take all of these experiences with you and maybe you do wake up in a whole new body with all this experience and get to be young again with all that you know. How incredible that will be. The possibilities were endless. We even wondered, "Do you think there are cities where you're going?"

BCM: *How extraordinary.*

DK: It was just an incredible night for me. And there was nothing to do but accept it and be with it. And as they say, the only way beyond the pain is through the pain.

BCM: *You get through by going through, because I've done it.*

DK: Right. And once we had gone through the painful part of it, the possibilities were endless and it became more a celebration of what was happening to him. When I thought about him going to this other place, maybe taking his experiences or maybe having a whole new body, I thought it's really the miracle of death. You know that you hear so much about the miracle of birth that no one thinks about what a miracle death must be.

BCM: *I did an interview with a woman who is a midwife to the dying. She talks about helping people through the dying process just as you help people midwife through the birthing process. Because it is a different type of birth. And that feels absolutely right to me.*

DK: Absolutely. And it was just an incredible night we had. You know I will cherish it my whole life. And it's interesting, Laurie, who is his nurse here, was telling him yesterday, "Joe, you have no idea how much you're helping me. I take care of so many people who won't talk about death. You're helping me so much by just letting me talk to you about it and being open about it." I told him he has no idea how unique he is that he's willing to talk about this.

BCM: *It sounds like an ideal death. A completion for both of you. It sounds to me like it's going to be just as beautiful and cherishing as both of you can possibly make it.*

DK: I was going to say exactly that. You know, It's going to be the saddest thing in the world for me, but as far as deaths go, this is going to be one of the greatest. It's amazing because as much as I deal with death, I've always thought, and it may be somewhat arrogant to say this, but I thought, "When it comes down to someone in my family, it will be so easy with all this experience." And now I look at that and think what a crazy thought, and I'm amazed at how hard it is. And as wonderful a transition as it is, it's just always going to be hard to say goodbye to someone you love.

When I walked into Joey's presence, he grinned at me and I smiled back at him. I knew that for however long Joey Shea was on this earth, I had found a dear friend. The room was full of joy, a luminous energy that I had experienced once before when my son was dying.

This energy of aliveness permeated the conversation that followed.

BCM: *It's great to see all of this energy here. Especially since I hear you're a performer, Joe. It's important to me to be able to talk with you like this because we all want to know more about how people really feel at this time in their lives.*

JS: Look, I can only tell you in two words. I'm ready. I've been everywhere, I've seen everything, I've had money, I've had none, I've lived a life. What a life! All I want to do is just go onward and see what it's going to be like over there.

BCM: *Sounds to me like you're an adventurer.*

JS: I certainly am. And look, I don't fear death. Are you kidding? If God took me off this earth this minute he'd be doing me a favor. I know, I've read too much. I've seen too much. I know, no one's going to kid me. There *is* life after death.

BCM: *I couldn't agree with you more, Joe.*

JS: And here's what I'm going to tell you. There's got to be life after death. There's got to be! When you die you go to a better place. You go to be with the ones you love. When we used to go to pray at a funeral I would stand there and I would know, the body was there, but the person had gone on. There was no one home! And all that was around that person, you know the air around that person, well, it's love. That air is love. I saw my friend in the coffin and I said, "He's sleeping, but he's still blessed." It was a blessing.

BCM: *Do you have an idea of what death will be for you? What do you think it's going to be like?*

JS: Well, how could life here on earth be any different from the hereafter? I go by one thing. What God does. So I want to talk about life, not death. Don't you think it's a miracle, two people get in bed?

BCM: *Oh, I do.*

JS: Wait a minute. People get in bed, they have sex, and it's a natural thing that they do, they both come together and they make a baby. Isn't it a miracle that that little stuff comes out of the penis and a baby is made? And that's *life*. And now I'll tell you what I think about death.

BCM: *What is it?*

JS: It's just this. There's no one going to cheat me out of my death.

BCM: *Good for you.*

JS: I can't wait.

DK: And it's interesting because there were so many times, in Sacramento when he was in the hospital when he wanted to talk about death, and people around didn't want to. You know? And he's entitled to this full experience. And to be around people who are willing to share it with him 100%. Scary, fun, good, bad.

BCM: *I wish you could have met my son Michael. You may meet him. He died a year and a half ago.*

JS: I might.

BCM: *And he died at home surrounded by his family and friends.*

JS: How old was he?

BCM: *He was twenty-eight. We were there for him and we loved him and we felt right about a lot of things, but at the same time we were not as prepared as we thought we would be. It hurt an awful lot. There were just an awful lot of devastating feelings going on. And when I see you and talk to you, I think, "This is a guy who knows what he's doing." And you seem so joyful, like you're just ready to rush into the experience.*

JS: Are you kidding? I wish it would happen right now. I'd like to close my eyes and that would be it. Because I want to tell ya, no one's kidding me. I've lived a fabulous life. There's nothing I missed in this world and all I can say is I'm not like the average person, the minute they get real sick and when they're old, they think they're going to die, they're calling the priest, they're calling the rabbi, they fear death. Not Joey Shea.

BCM: *That's the difference. You're not fearing the next experience, you're just...almost like a kid in a candy store.*

JS: Did you meet Mabel?

BCM: *I did meet Mabel. I did. What do you think it's going to be like on the other side, Joe?*

JS: It's going to be more beautiful than it's ever been here. It's really going to be wonderful.

BCM: *You going to be dancing?*

JS: Well, stuff like that I can't prophesy. I can't say nothing like that. But, I do know one thing, that the minute you die your spirit leaves you and I do know that there is life after death. A thousand to one greatest professors in America have proven life after death. And who are they to be wrong?

BCM: *Not only that, but there are so many people who have seen the other side and then come back from near-death experiences. Have you read some of those experiences?*

JS: I sure have.

BCM: *Have you ever gone through an experience where you did perhaps see the light or go through the tunnel or is that something that's just around the corner for you?*

JS: Well, I tell you, there was one time, I lost a brother. He was nineteen years old. Strangest death in the world. Never sick a day in his life. Two o'clock in the morning he stopped off in this place and had two hot dogs. And he got deathly sick and they rushed him to the hospital. You would never believe what I'm going to tell you. A wheel fell off the ambulance. They didn't make it to the hospital. He died. That brother came to me in my dreams.

BCM: *When?*

JS: While I was sleeping.

BCM: *I know, was this right after he died, or just recently?*

JS: Oh no, no, no. This is long after he died. And he was talking to me.

BCM: *And what did he tell you?*

JS: Well, between you and I, there's a lot of things we talked about that has left my mind and all that, but, I'm just trying to tell you I had an experience with a death too.

BCM: *Yes, I hear that.*

DK: And you know in making this choice, there *was* a choice. The background on this is that Joey had had a major heart attack and went in the hospital and recovered real well. And then he got out and within a day was sick again. So he went back in, and that's when they also found the cancer. And it looks like the cancer has been there for a while, and chances are at this point that it probably has spread. So they gave us the choice of either doing nothing, which they had no trouble saying that they didn't believe in, or two, giving him what's called a Lubiliostomy, like a colostomy bag, which would give him maybe two to three more months, and my response to that was out of those two to three more months, these are the things that are important to my father: traveling, doing shows, being active. How many of those things will he be able to do? And they said, "Well, probably none. He'll probably be at home." And I said, "Are we talking about two to three more months of hospital visits, infections, problems?" And they said, "Well, most likely." And then they said, "In two months his heart will be even more recovered and we can probably do a third surgery to try and get the cancer out. But we'd have to see if it'd be possible. Whether we think he could recover from that." And we really had to look at the difference between quality of life and quantity of life, in that I just couldn't see his last days consisting of this tube, that bag, this hospital, that doctor's visit. When my mother passed away she had so many tubes. There was no dignity to it at all.

BCM: *But you knew to ask the right questions. Joe is not going to let anybody else tell him what to do with his life.*

DK: Absolutely. Let me tell you something the doctor did that I got very upset with. The doctor said to me one morning, "Your father has informed me surgery will be okay." And I said, "I can't believe this, you talked to him?" And the doctor said,

"Yes." And I said, "Well I'd like to hear it from him." And the doctor went in and said, "Mr. Sheavitz, you want to feel better, don't you?" And my father said, "Yeah." So the doctor said, "Well, if we could make you feel better with surgery, wouldn't that be great?" And my father said, "Yeah." And I said to the doctor, "You consider that an informed consent?" I was furious. I said to the doctor, "You need to spell out to him what life will be like for him either way."

JS: There's the obstacle now. David don't want it to happen to me like it did to two people that I love dearly. My dad went through what they wanted me to go through. They wanted to operate and they wanted to make an incision like they made on my dad. For two years he just sat like this (slumps) in the kitchen in the Jewish ghetto with my mother, and I was in show business. I used to fly home all the time, and it killed me to see how this man suffered. Now that's one thing *I* got to go through? No! So my son came to me one day, not too long ago, and said, "Dad, I filled out some certain papers and I want you to sign them. Dad, do you want us to suffer the enormous pain we all suffered when Mom was dying?" For four years my wife was in intensive care. Every gadget in the world on her. I had her in front of four doctors at this hospital in New Orleans before she later went to a different hospital. And I was paying from $200 to $220 to $230 a day. Way back then. It's more now, of course. One day we were driving downtown in my car, and she had an attack. I rushed her to the hospital. Only a small city of 105,000. They did not have a dialysis machine. And they advised me to run her real quick over to Freedman, in New Orleans, which was seventy-two miles and would take over forty or fifty minutes. And I got her over there.

DK: But they hooked her up to every machine conceivable, and every tube conceivable, and the thing is that we were only allowed to see her in intensive care for five minutes every two hours. Because the family is such an interference.

JS: I didn't tell you the bottom line, that the last year in intensive care she was in a coma. Couldn't recognize him or me. I put her on the second floor in a private room. She could not make the dialysis machine, she was too weak. So I put her in this private room. We stayed in Howard Johnson's Hotel. And five minutes every two hours we went up to her bedside, and never was there a time in those five minutes that two of the doctors weren't there. They never let us see her alone.

BCM: *You didn't have any privacy.*

DK: Right.

JS: Now listen, when we walked out to take the elevator downstairs, they said to us hundreds of times, "Mr. Sheavitz," — that's my regular name for tax purposes, my show name is Joey Shea — "Mr. Sheavitz, why don't you want us to pull the plug? If she survives she's going to be a vegetable. We don't need your money." But one day I was talking with some other doctors, they walked out in the hall with me and they said the same thing the other two doctors had. They said, "How long are you going to let this poor soul go on? Why don't you let her go?" I never answered nobody in all them years. But you know what happened then? I turned around and I said, "Doctor, you are right. I am ready to let her go." Then when we got downstairs, over the speaker came this message, "Mr. Sheavitz, you're wanted in the nearest station office." And they told me. She was gone. Finally at peace. Now my son talked to me not too long ago when I got sick. I'm talking about six months ago. I was always in perfect health. He says to me, "Dad, I don't never want to see you going through what Mom went through." He says, "Will it be all right with you?" It's all right with me. "Would you want to go peacefully?" I said, "You better believe it."

BCM: *I'm signing those papers myself because I believe the same way you do. You're talking about the Living Will, aren't you? (See the appendix for the text of* The Living Will *and* The Durable Power of Attorney for Health Care. *-ed.)*

DK: Right. And you know the thing I was going to say about seeing her five minutes every two hours is that when we went up there, when she had died, and you know after someone dies you remove all the tubes, I just thanked God that we could finally see her body at peace.

BCM: *At peace. That's the word, at peace.*

DK: Because, you know, there was a tube everywhere there could be a tube. It wasn't my mother at that point. And when they finally pulled it out, what a relief to know that that was how it should be.

JS: Nobody wants to accept death.

BCM: *That was the question I was going to ask you.*

JS: I think it's the most wonderful thing in the world. I can't wait.

BCM: *Do you think that is the most important thing you would really like to tell people? Because you're going to live forever in this book, Joey. I'm going to put down everything you say so that other sons like David and mothers like me, can really see how it can be. So I want to know what other words of wisdom you have for those of us who are facing death. Because we all lose our parents, we all lose our husbands or wives or children or other people that we love.*

JS: I lost the greatest parents in the world.

BCM: *You did?*

JS: I lost the greatest, greatest wife in the world. And I want to tell you right now, I can't wait till we're set to go into the next world. I can't wait. If it happened in the next five minutes I'd be the happiest man in the world.

DK: And the thing that I've gotten from him that is so important is that it's *okay* to die.

BCM: *That's such a big step because don't you think most people fear death so much they just keep holding it away and holding it away? How can you get on with your life if you're fearing what's around the next corner?*

DK: And even when they were talking to me about making the decisions about him, when he wasn't doing as well up there, and he wasn't able to actively make those decisions, first of all, I was amazed at how they weren't really even willing to honor the Living Will that much. And how aggressive they wanted to be.

BCM: *And you're very much more skilled in how hospitals work and how it all works. What about the civilians here, what about these poor people that come in and don't know any better and just do what the doctor says?*

DK: I said to the doctor, "Are you telling me that if I didn't have the medical knowledge, I might have flown up here and the next thing I would know is I would end up with this 'thing' in a nursing home that's had a stroke on the surgery table and a colostomy, and this decision would have been made already?" And he said, "The reality is, it would have been made." So what kind of quality of life would my father have if I hadn't been there to say, "Well, wait a minute, I know what the reality is. Sure, surgery can help, but, what kind of life will Joe have?" If I wasn't a nurse, I don't know what it would have been like. I just thank God I do have more knowledge.

BCM: *You are saying loud and clear that there are alternatives, that you can choose, that you really have to fight for your right to go out of this world with love and dignity. You have to fight for your rights to be treated as a human being, not as a dying 'thing.' This has been a very recent thing for patients and their families to even know that they had a right, much less the doctors allow them to be a part of the mystery process surrounding hospitals and illnesses.*

DK: But you know it was so hard for me trying to make that decision and argue with everyone. I was constantly talking to a friend of mine, asking for help, for reassurance.

JS: It was hard for him.

BCM: *I know how hard it was for him.*

DK: And there were three doctors there who had a whole separate belief system than me. And to argue with these doctors was almost impossible. They couldn't believe my point of view. I kept calling a friend of mine who's a physician, who's now Joey's physician down here. Every night I cried on the phone to him saying, "I can't *believe* this. I feel like a voice screaming and no one can hear me. Because they don't seem to understand." And it was such a hard decision to make because I thought, "I would love to have him with me forever and ever."

BCM: *Who wouldn't? Hey, I'd like to have you around for a good long time, Joe. And I just met you.*

DK: But I thought, how selfish it would be of me to want him to have less than one hundred percent of life. That would be selfish on my part, as much as my heart says I would love to. You know, there's a part of me that would love to even have him be in a nursing home. To have him on any terms. There's another part of me that just wants him to have it all or to have nothing. And if there's nothing left here, then to go on to something else elsewhere.

BCM: *Do people try to make you feel guilty?*

DK: Well, let me tell you, they sure do! There was one doctor who told me what I was doing was inhumane. Really!

BCM: *You're under such stress anyway and having such conflicting feelings at this time.*

JS: It's *his* father. It's *his* flesh and blood. He has the right.

BCM: *That's right. His love gives him that right.*

DK: There was another doctor that I actually fired from his case.

JS: You know what that doctor said to me?

BCM: *What?*

JS: When he walked into the hospital he wanted to check me out for the last time. He says to me, real snotty, "You know your son fired me." Ohhh! What that did to his dignity!

BCM: *He wasn't Mr. Omnipotent.*

DK: Right. And this doctor was seventy-five years old, one of the founding fathers of this hospital, and one morning in intensive care, I told him I wanted my father to be a 'no-code,' which means I don't want him to be resuscitated if something happens. And he said to me, "Are those *your* wishes or your father's?"

BCM: *Like you're going to run around stabbing your father or something like this.*

DK: And I said, "They're my father's wishes first and they're *my* wishes second." And then he said, "Well, I think you've been influencing your father." And I said, "I would hope so. I would hope as a son I have some influence on my father and second, as a nurse I would hope I would have some influence on my father. And besides that," I told him, "My word doesn't really matter here in the sense that my father has made out a Living Will." The doctor then asked me, "Could I see it?" I told him it was in Los Angeles. Then he said, "Well, until you get it I feel like you have no rights." So I said, "You will actually have me fly back to L.A. to get this piece of paper to prove it?" And he said, "When *I'm* eighty-three years old I want to be a full-code."

BCM: *He doesn't know till he gets there.*

DK: I kept talking to him. I told him, "Wouldn't it be the worst experience of your life if you had decided that, and a stranger walked into your life with a different belief system and tried to get you to change your beliefs? Wouldn't that be the worst thing that could happen? You've only known my father for a few weeks. How could you say on any level that you have any more rights than I do as his son?"

JS: He really told that doctor off.

BCM: *You've brought up a son who's very loving, very coura-*
geous and very clear. Most of us have so many layers
of perceptions and belief systems that when the death
of a loved one hits us, when we feel we might be losing
someone we love, everything in our society reinforces
the separation instead of it being a chance for more love
to be expressed. More communion is really the word
I'm thinking of, between one another. I think some-
times we let the fears of the doctors get in the way. The
people who are playing God out there.

DK: Absolutely. And I don't think my father and I
        have ever been closer than we are now.

JS: Never.

BCM: *Well, do you think you're going to see your Dad after*
he goes?

JS: Yes.

DK: Yeah, absolutely.

JS: And I believe I'm going to see David too.

DK: And I'll tell you, we have something together that
        we both believe in. It's like the other day when
        my father said, "I was just thinking of your
        Mom." I have a belief that all of a sudden there
        will be a time when I'll be walking around and I'll
        be real busy with my life and he'll be gone, and
        out of the blue for no reason he'll pop into my
        mind, and I'll know at that moment wherever he
        is, he's thinking of me.

BCM: *I feel closer to Michael in many ways, although we*
were very, very close in the years just preceding his
death, because once he came to me after his death and
told me that whenever I felt a cool breeze on my cheek
that felt like a kiss, that it was him saying hello. I
thought, ''Oh, how wonderful.'' So it's really easy for

me to talk to his picture at night and say, "Michael, now, I really had a tough day and how can I get the messages out that you wanted, and how can I do the books? Come on, give me some advice here." I'm asking advice! I'd never ask advice of him when he was alive. I'm asking advice of my twenty-eight year-old son who has passed on. Imagine!

DK: Yes. The other thing that we talked about that night in intensive care is an experience of my best friend, my dearest friend, Steve Oldfield. He said that he dreamed one night about his own death and that he thought the hardest thing about his death when it came down to that moment would be letting go of the people he loves.

BCM: *I agree.*

DK: And then he said that he realized in that dream that the place where he was going was a place where they already were.

BCM: *That's very profound.*

DK: In the sense that we talked about earlier, you know my father might go to another place and find out that I exist there too on another level.

BCM: *You've just got to be careful what you're doing, David, because if your father is looking over your shoulder from the other side, you ought to make really sure that you behave yourself. (Laughter).*

JS: That's right. He loves me. Anybody that would tell a lie on their deathbed isn't good. And I want to tell you, I know I come on with all this real fast. I didn't get sick until about six months ago. And you know how it started?

BCM: *How?*

JS: I had a dream. I had a dream David was standing over my grave, and the fella he just talked about,

Steve Oldfield, had his arm around him. My son was crying something terrible, and Steve says to him, "David, it's all right. Your father, if he's got to go, he's had a wonderful life." And I told my son, "That's right. I've done everything I wanted to do in my life." I was a great showman, lady.

BCM: *You were a great showman? What did you do?*

JS: I was a comedian and singer and one of the best in America.

BCM: *Who did you play with?*

JS: Just myself, I was a comedian singer like Bob Hope.

BCM: *But I mean did you play on certain bills?*

DK: Tell her who you started out with.

BCM: *Who did you start out with?*

JS: I started out in 1924. I was a singer around the way of George Burns. With a piano player. I was discovered out in the audience and this agent put me into show business. And from '26 to '42 I was in show business until Uncle Sam came along. We was at war with Hitler. I had just turned thirty-eight years old, and I was a tough comedian playing with the best. And I got my notice from the government, I was drafted. And they told me in Chicago, everybody knew me there, and they wanted to know if I was born in Chicago or somewhere else. I said, "No, Providence, Rhode Island." And they told me, "Go to work, get your agent and manager and take ninety days to settle up your affairs, then report to your draft board in Providence, Rhode Island. And if you report to the draft board in Providence, Rhode Island that means that you'll have a chance to take any branch of service you want. But if we draft you cold-blooded right here in Chicago, we're going to send you down south to the Army and infantry." But you want to know something? My manager finally sent me to help in the war, and I finished my show business career in the war. I was really proud of it. I never had to report to the draft board because they came and destroyed Hitler. And I went and opened up my own club down south for twenty-eight years. I had a great career. Wait till you hear one of my tapes.

BCM: *I'd love to hear your tapes.*

DK: I heard that cue.

BCM: *But I'm wondering, Joey, I don't want to talk too long to tire you out, but I'm also so fascinated with everything that you've been telling me.*

JS: You know, I want to tell you something. See me talking like I do. It kind of hurts me in my throat now talking so much.

BCM: *You think we've been talking too long?*

JS: Well I have. But I want to say one more thing to you, young lady, and it's important.

BCM: *I'm listening.*

JS: You tell them all out there what I said. I have looked death in the face and I say, "Wow! Death is a great adventure. I can hardly wait."

Joey Shea died peacefully five days later.

The Gift
of
the
Generations

*The wise and knowing part, vastly in tune with life,
brings its wisdom to mother/grandmother and says,
"This is the stuff character is made of. . ."*

*Once life is conceived, its entire rhythm is to be experi-
enced. Breathe deeply; learn to flow with it. The great
pain of your labor will be followed by the incredible beauty
and joy of new life.*

*The age old wisdom comes to us from every direction.
Yesterday I buried my daughter and grandchild. Happily,
today a man tells me of the birth of a new child and I
smile at him with love. He has thus assured me of the
continuity of life.*

CAROL W. PARRISH-HARRA
A New Age Handbook On Death And Dying

2

Helen Thomas Cook is a seventy-two year-old great-grandmother from Texas whose insights on grieving through the generations, what she calls "The Train Through Life and Death," have a poignancy and wisdom distilled from years of living. Her life is a gift to me and to all who know her.

The Train Through Life and Death

I had to say good-bye to an old friend today. He was 112 years old, and I had known him for sixteen real years, since he was a small black puppy of six months, with a white streak on his head, and a heart that loved me unconditionally. He was not my dog. He belonged to my daughter and her husband; but she told me she always knew when my car turned the corner into her street, because Happy would run to the door to look for me. Today, I looked into his loyal eyes, lifted him off of his tottering legs and hugged him before putting him into the waiting arms of a man from the Humane Society. I had made the only decision possible for him, but that little friend represented a whole era in the life of my family, full of joy as well as bitterness and regret. I cried for him.

I needed those tears. I needed to grieve for my grandson who died eighteen months ago, and my sister who died a year ago. I had not been able to cry, and that left me tied into a hard knot. I felt that I had been holding my breath for so long that my body was stiff and unyielding, afraid to let go and let the tears wash away the grief, the anguish, the loneliness, the guilt — all the hurting feelings that beset us when we lose someone we love.

My grandson Michael died of AIDS, and I watched his life prolonged beyond reason with suffering. I wanted to gather him up into my arms like a little child, and hold him against all hurt, all pain, all uncertainty in his mind. But all I could do was to help him pass the hours and the days with stories of the years when he was a young boy and relive the memories we had of happy times together. He would go back to those years over and over, so we relived them together, so he could forget the dreadful present.

My sister Betty was an alcoholic, and we had a hard time understanding each other during the last ten years of her life. In my inner strength and zeal, I could not imagine what could lead anyone to destroy their body and their mind with alcohol. I know I do not truly understand this disease, and I felt guilty because I could not fill her great need for someone to be beside her and encourage her. Yet, like so many of us, she really wanted to be alone. It bothered her to have a 'watchdog' monitoring her every act. I am glad to say that we had many shared weekends of fun and companionship during the past few years, as we visited and played lots of card games, and enjoyed each other more than we ever had in years past. Yet I could not cry for Betty; and with her, too, I played the game of, "Do you remember when?"

It seems to be always the past that helps us to bear the troubles and sorrows of the present. So I took to my past to explain some of my inability to shed tears.

When asked in my seventies to think back on how I faced grief in my lifetime, I must go back to the first funeral that I remember. Picture, if you will, a small active girl of about seven years, black hair in a Dutch bob. She is wearing a maroon velveteen dress trimmed with braid, and her sister Dorothy, a few years older, wears an identical dress in dark green. They are too warm for the early spring day, but the dresses were gifts brought from Chicago by the grandfather who is being buried today. I do not quite understand when I see a great-aunt suddenly burst into tears and just as suddenly avert her face and stiffen her narrow shoulders as she silently wipes her face on a lace-edged handkerchief. The funeral itself is an innovation in our lives, and the arrival at the old country cemetery a whole new adventure.

I do not know my grandfather very well, for he does not live with my grandmother; but the feelings I can sense in my mother and her sister, the aunts and uncles who are my grandfather's children, as hard as that is to imagine, all combine to fill me with an urge to cry as my mother is crying. But my grandmother is standing behind me, her long fingers steady on my shoulders. When I look up at her, I cannot find the soft twinkle in her eyes that always meet mine. Today, she stares across the cemetery, looking away from all that is going on, her face as stony as the headstones around us. I want to cry out, but those fingers hold me still, captured by her stony grief.

I was only in my late thirties when I lost my husband. Dare I go back to that time, so far away, to resurrect that other lifetime? It is as if forgetting that time in my life will make the pain go away. John was seven years older than I, and we met when I was only fourteen, but waited to be married three days before I became eighteen. He spoiled me, loved me, left me a legacy of a gentle man, the father of my three daughters. When he died, after a long illness, I felt pressured by all I had to do, to keep the funeral plans, sleeping arrangements, meals and baby-sitting all coordinated for that week, so that none of the family and friends would have to worry about anything. It was as if I grabbed all those plans and made them mine, because I was so good at details. I was not good at loss and grieving. I had cried all my tears the year before when the doctor told me that John could not live out the year, possibly only three or four months. That first night, I buried John several times, grieving and picking out pall bearers and telling the children. The night was filled with all my weeping, so that the next morning and for more than another year, I was able to face and take care of the mundane part of my life, putting aside the grief.

Sometimes, I can't remember how he looked or the way his voice sounded, and I panic! And then, the few times he has come to me in dreams, we have neither of us become any older. His picture on the dresser in my bedroom faces me, his eyes so warm and brown, crinkling at the corners, his smile, those perfect teeth, his voice enclosing me in safety and love. But I feel that must have been in another lifetime. We exist together only in memories, only in the past. He is just waiting for me.

I am very active in the present, but I am ruled in many ways by the past. As with Michael, and my sister, and my husband, we shared memories that made grief bearable, although sometimes unexpressed.

With my mother, it was different. I believe we were more like twins than mother and daughter. There was a special affinity between us. So much of our feelings, thoughts, and beliefs were the same. There were many times when we knew instinctively what the other was thinking or was going to say. We could sit in companionable silence, tuned in to the same wave length of thoughts. Losing her to death was like a part of me dying.

On a hot summer night after she died, I could hear the telephone ringing and ringing next door in my mother's empty house. I could cover my ears and sob into my pillow, but the ringing would still be there inside my head. By rigidly suiting my manner to that of the generations before me, I could keep my chin up and my eyes dry among others, but every night, alone, my heart would continue breaking.

One cold winter evening, arriving home in the early dark, a great wave of grief enveloped me as I groped for the garage door, in the shadow of the empty house next door. My mother had always turned on her backyard light for me and tapped on her back room window to let me know she was watching out for my safety. I knew, then, that she had been with me in so many ways that I could never lose her again, although the hurt will always be there. It is the little things, the sudden ways that life's events remind us of the great love we had, that makes us want to run to our mother's arms, and be a child once more, so snug, so safe.

On one Thanksgiving Day, a holiday my mother always loved, I was missing her warmth and her humor and her little laugh. And I recalled so many drives we had made up to that little north Texas town to visit the two great-aunts. And while I thought about it, I was certain my mother was having Thanksgiving dinner with the aunts, in Heaven, laughing and talking and enjoying one another as they always did.

Traditions in the holidays go on as usual. I carefully unwrap the tiny wax turkeys and Indians and Pilgrims to grace the Thanksgiving table, at whichever house we are gathering that year. The wrappings are threadbare and falling apart, just an old white grocery sack I could replace easily with a new strong one. But this sack is different. This one has my mother's distinctive, almost unreadable handwriting on it, indicating that Indians and Pilgrims dwell within.

Sometimes I see a glimpse of our whole family, from its earliest years, as in a railroad station, figures only dimly seen and unrecognizable in the mist and shadows. But there is a constant movement as trains come and go: passengers getting off of trains, others getting on. The new babies are handed off the train to eager waiting arms; those who are leaving are getting on the train. Yet there is no rush. All know where they are going, at their appointed time. It is a joy to see a new young face. It is doubly a joy to get on the train and greet an old familiar one.

How close we are to those others who precede us into Heaven! There are cords between us, sensitive and unseen, yet stronger than Death, stronger than Life itself, as strong as Love and Faith.

Yet I have faced grief so many times and have seldom been granted the blessing of tears. I am still that child standing in the winds of a country cemetery. There are silent stern faces above and around me, my Grandmother's strong restraining hands on my shoulders that have kept me wrapped in a wall of coldness against Death. I have seldom been able to break down that barrier.

I wish they had let me cry. I wish they had told me it was all right. But thanks to a dear old black dog, today I cried.

The Gift
of
Honesty

THE DYING PERSON'S BILL OF RIGHTS

The right to be treated as a living human being until death.

The right to have a sense of hopefulness, however changing its focus may be.

The right to be cared for by those who can maintain a sense of hopefulness, however changing this may be.

The right to express feelings and emotions about their own approaching death in their own way.

The right to participate in decisions concerning their own care.

The right to expect continuing medical and nursing care even though the "cure" goals may be changed to "comfort" goals.

The right not to die alone.

The right to be free of pain.

The right to have questions answered fully, and honestly.

The right to retain their own individuality and not be judged for decisions which may be contrary to beliefs of others.

The right to be cared for by caring, sensitive, knowledgeable people who will attempt to understand their needs.

The right to die in peace and dignity.

The right to expect that the sanctity of the human body will be respected after death.

— From *Home Care: A Practical Alternative To Extended Hospitalization*
By E.M. BAULCH

3

Bill Hodgson is an AIDS home health care specialist who has worked for several home health care
agencies.

With candor and honesty, this open, smiling young
man talked about his first experience in working with
a dying patient and how it changed his life. He spoke,
too, of what he calls "a healthy way of dying," and of
the Dying Person's Bill of Rights.

BCM: *Well, the first thing that I want to ask you is what led
you to become a nurse/caregiver for the terminally ill,
especially for AIDS patients?*

BH: That's a good question in itself. When I gradu-
ated from nursing school in 1981, I had been
working in emergency medicine nursing, that
was my specialty. And I continued on working in
the emergency room both in St. Francis Hospital
and then Kaiser Hollywood, and then Kaiser
West L.A., seeing a number of different emergency type cases. I saw trauma, and I saw medical problems. Well, at the same time I began to
see the number of patients coming in who were
diagnosed with AIDS. Now you have to look at
this in conjunction with the fact that I lived in
West Hollywood, and I'm gay, so I was in a gay

community and was beginning, just beginning, back in 1982, '83, to be learning a little bit more about AIDS, and hearing horror stories of people who were being diagnosed with it. So I was working in the emergency room and what I was seeing was something that disturbed me. And that was the care that the AIDS patients were getting when they came in the emergency room. At that time, not many people knew a lot about AIDS, but they *did* know that it was contagious in some way and they knew that people were dying. And it was such a sensation in the beginning. So we put our patients in a little room and put an isolation sign all over the door and didn't allow them any visitors, and didn't allow anything more than minimal contact with any emergency room personnel or any other hospital personnel. And very few people wanted to go near the room. This was disturbing to me on a personal basis as well as on a professional basis. Professionally, being a nurse, I just couldn't understand how people could differentiate caring for one group of people and not for another.

BCM: *Good point.*

BH: On a personal level I thought, "Wait a minute, most of these people that are coming in are young gay guys and I'm a young gay guy. I could be in the same situation they're in." So I was taking this very personally too. And that is what I was watching happen. So I decided that it was time for me to leave the emergency room setting and do something that was more committed to serving those with AIDS. I was learning about the disease myself. I was reading all that I could, listening to the different types of media approaches from the newspapers, magazines, television and radio, and learning about it. And I decided that I wanted to help people, but I didn't want to do it in a hospital setting. So the alternative became home health care. And that was an area that was just beginning, essentially. This was in early 1984 that I decided to work in this area. It was a new area. There wasn't a lot of terminal home care going on. Home care pretty much was taking care of older people, going in for quick treatments, doing what you needed to do and leaving.

BCM: *Was it offered just for people dying at home, the very elderly? Or was there hardly any home care available at all?*

BH: There wasn't a lot of home care at that time directed towards the dying, the hospice type process. Most home care was directed towards chronic illness. Not necessarily with an emphasis on the death and dying part of it. The aggressive, acute types of treatments still had to go into the hospital. Very few patients would stay home.

BCM: *And most people didn't have an alternative to dying in the hospital. It was the hospital or nothing?*

BH: It was the hospital or you were pretty much on your own. That's right. You could rely on your family, your friends, your loved ones, but you couldn't really rely on any input from the medical system for the most part, at least not that I saw, from what I was exposed to. And so, it was interesting because I decided I wanted to start working in the home but I certainly didn't know what to do. There were two agencies that I knew of at that time that were just beginning to work in that area of care. I went and interviewed with

one of them. I started working for one of them
and almost immediately I was working in a home
on my first case! And it was just amazing to me
because I had never seen anything like this before. I remember the first patient I worked with,
I went into the home and he was getting very
close to dying. I could tell by the look of him, by
the look on his face. And I have very sharply at-
tuned sensing skills because I came from all the
emergency room experience. So I looked and I
thought, "This man's dying." And all the training
that I'd always had was, well, he shouldn't be
here, he should be in a hospital if he's this close
to death. He was so uncomfortable, he was having difficulty breathing and he was weak, he was
in pain. There were a lot of things going on with
him.

BCM: *Was he alone, or did he have help?*

BH: A nursing situation was already in place, so I
came on as a relief nurse, and he also did have a
supporting network of friends around him. So he
was not alone. And, my first impression, once
the nurse that I relieved left, was that I needed to
call the agency and arrange for this person to get
to a hospital because he was just too sick. So I
called the nursing director and he said, "I know
you're new at this, Bill, and I can see you don't
understand the philosophy of what we're doing
here. He knows he's dying. His friends know he's
dying. We know he's dying. And that's why he's
opted for staying home and the emphasis here is
not to get him back into the hospital, but to make
him as comfortable as we can so that he has a certain quality of life during this dying process."

BCM: *What were your feelings?*

BH: My feelings were helplessness. I wanted to do something concrete, something tangible.

BCM: *Fix it, make it well.*

BH: That was my primary concern. And I thought there must be something that I can do, some medicine to give, some treatment, not that's going to cure the disease, not something that's going to make him better, but there must be something that at the very least will help him out of what appears to be a very uncomfortable situation. Well, I've since learned that there certainly *are* things we as caregivers can do within the dying process to provide comfort. Anyway, this patient didn't follow the 'ideal textbook case' as far as bypassing the unpleasant part of dying and going peacefully. Because he never accepted the dying process. He fought it. And I'll never forget how terrified I was because he was having a lot of confusion due to lack of oxygen. That was physiological and I knew that. But he also was not going to accept death at all. He was going to fight with every ounce of strength that he had. And this man was so weak that I couldn't believe that he could even pull himself up off the bed.

BCM: *How old was he?*

BH: I think late thirties, approximately, is how old he was. But that entire night he would not lie down because he knew if he lay down he would die. I just know that he knew that, even though he could not communicate that verbally. So he made himself sit up on the edge of the bed the entire night. And I was terrified. I wanted to do something, but there was nothing I could do. I would try and help him to lie down and he would lie for a few seconds and then jump right back up again. Because he didn't want to go to sleep. He didn't want to close his eyes. Finally he was exhausted. He could not hold himself up anymore and he had to lie down and rest. He went to sleep. And this was just about at seven in the morning, I was going off, another nurse coming on, and he did die about two hours later. This was my first experience with home care, and my first real experience with a home setting for death.

BCM: *Had you seen people die before in the hospitals?*

BH: Many times in the emergency room. Many times. From heart attacks, from trauma. But it is so much more clinical. In the emergency room you are moving so quickly, so fast, you're doing so many things, that although it affects you, it didn't affect me nearly in the same way as it did being one-on-one in a quiet place like a home, watching this process occur.

BCM: *Did you feel like your presence was helpful to him even though he was struggling with the letting go process?*

BH: I think I was so new to it then that I was self-obsessed with my own fear.

BCM: *Thank you for being honest.*

BH: I really never knew if I was the help I wanted to be to him. I cared very much and my focus was making him comfortable, and I felt like I wasn't making him comfortable, and I was racking my brains the whole night trying to figure out what I could do to make him more comfortable. I was thinking of me a lot, and thinking of how best to help *him* secondarily. And it never worked. So it was a very traumatic experience for me. And I cried and cried the next day when he died. And I thought, "Maybe I just shouldn't be in this field, maybe this is all wrong."

BCM: *I can understand your momentary feelings at that time.*

BH: I thought, "Maybe I better go back to the emergency room again, something I know I can deal with." The nursing director was smart and he knew how this affected me personally. He made me come into the office and made me sit down with him and go over how this affected me, and what I felt. Talk about it. Vocalize it. That was really a lesson he taught me about stress management. Not to keep it in. I let it out. I talked about it. I expressed all my feelings and I put that whole experience in perspective. And getting perspective is a valuable lesson too, which I still apply now. I did other home care work after that and it was never as difficult as that first time. It still hurts, though. I just can't think how many times I've been with a patient in the home and for no reason at all, just in watching what's occurring, whatever process might be going on right at that moment, I start crying. And it's just feeling, that's all that it is, plain and simple as that, coming up, and it's overwhelming and I start crying. And I always try and maintain my composure very quickly because it isn't always appropriate to indulge in your own emotions. Sometimes you need to be the one in control.

BCM: *And sometimes you need to just express your feelings and that person can know that you are there for them.*

BH: I've done that too, yes. That can be okay. As it turned out, very shortly after that my nursing director asked me if I would consider coming in the office and working with him on case management.

BH: And I said, "Well I really don't have much experience in home care but I would be glad to learn." And he taught me the way his office worked. And I began having exposure to blind patients, and management cases and a lot of patients.

BCM: *When you were going into the home, how did you deal with the families or friends who were there?*

BH: My approach has always been that when I go in the home I just want to be myself. I want to be honest and open and just myself. I've seen too many other people come in that for some reason, I don't what their reason is but I know that I've seen it and I don't like it, feel that they need to put on an air of superiority in whatever their field is medically. I think maybe sometimes it's to keep that detachment we're supposed to have.

BCM: *Because many of us in our culture are so afraid of death, anyway, is that it? So as a professional you're supposed to back off and keep your barriers up?*

BH: To back off. And I just feel like I'm going to be the best help to the family, the friend, the patient, whoever's involved, if I can sit down and I can make them comfortable with the fact that I'm just a person. "I know some nursing and I'm here to help you with what I know. And if you can trust me a little bit, well, then I think I can be a good resource for you. If you want me to back off or go away, then I'll do that too." It's the honesty and the openness that I pride myself on most. With the family and with the friends. Generally speaking there has been an overwhelming positive response from them. Yet there are some situations that are no-win situations, where people are having such a difficult time dealing with their own emotions and being honest about their own feelings that I don't think that it would really matter what I said or what I did. They just have to go through it.

BCM: *But just being there for them in honesty. That is the key.*

BH: Ultimately that helps. Sometimes it doesn't help; sometimes even my presence is rejected. Then it doesn't even matter if I am there or not. In those cases I respect that situation and I just leave.

BCM: *So when you see a patient who is at the point of dying you just work on intuition and setting up a trusting situation?*

BH: A great deal of it is on intuition, feeling what the person wants. The patients I've seen go through so many different stages. In each minute it changes.

BCM: *So all those stages that Elizabeth Kubler-Ross talks about can happen in five or ten minutes, right? The denial part, the anger, the grief, the guilt?*

BH: It's certainly not in order. And yes, they can happen like that, all at once, all mixed up. Or some people will focus on just a few of the feelings. That's what I have seen. So I play it by ear, just discerning what the needs are of everybody that's involved. Because everybody is equally important in the dying process.

BCM: *Yes. That's true.*

BH: The last patient that I took care of had gone back home to live with his family. He lived with his mother and his brother's daughter. Then he had two sisters that were there every day and a great network of people. As well as me taking care of Michael, that was his name. I know that was your son's name too.

BCM: *Yes, and our family took care of Michael until he died.*

We had great help from visiting nurses, Shanti, and hospice.

BH: So *this* Michael (not your Michael, BettyClare, but my Michael, this young man), his mother was with him, his sisters, his brother, everybody was always around. Sometimes I had to ask them not to be around so much because of what it was doing to him. He was always my primary focus, his comfort; but of equal importance to me were the needs of the family that lived there. That was my job. That was why I was there. And I paid close attention to what everybody needed during this entire dying process. And I emphasize this when I'm interviewing nurses who want to work in the home. Most of my initial interview I cover the clinical aspects. I ask, "Are you good clinically, are you emotionally and psychologically supportive?" I talk about the interaction with the patient. But I spend as much time talking about how they will interact with whatever significant others may be there. Because that is equally important.

BCM: *So* caring *is more important than any technical efficiency?*

BH: The efficiency is certainly very important, but anybody can learn to do skillful nursing. Anybody can learn to do the technical nursing. But the caring, that's what separates the very loving health care workers that are helping a patient and a family through the dying process at home, as opposed to a technical nurse that can come in and give the drug treatment and therapies and turn the patient.

BCM: *I remember we were so delighted with the help that we received, because we'd been doing things in shifts that seemed to be twenty-four hours long, and we were impressed with everyone except one attendant and that one person did not have the love, the commitment. It felt like that one person did not care, that it was a job instead of a commitment to this whole work.*

BH: I have seen that happen.

BCM: *Do you do anything "special" to assist the family in coming to terms with what's happening or do you just play it by ear?*

BH: The only thing I think is special is just addressing the issues and needs of *both* the patient and his family because I see so many others just not paying attention to the family. Certainly we have resources such as Mothers of AIDS Patients, resources available to give to families if they're interested. But primarily, I've been focused on just being there for the family and friends. They need somebody to sit down with who's a professional, so they can ask the technical questions. And they also need somebody to sit down with who is objective and will listen and care. I can do both, you know, but the main thing is that they have resources like that available to them, on hand when they need it. So much of it is just listening.

BCM: *What about when either the family or the person denies that they are going to die? Are there ways that you can assist?*

BH: That is so tough, and that has to be taken care of so individually.

BCM: *What works better? I mean from your experience, what can the family do in the situation? Or what can the dying person do? What can we all do in that situation to heal ourselves or clear the way?*

BH: I almost wish that people could face it head on. Certainly I can't understand how anyone can come to be with their son or daughter and sit with the patient and see the deterioration, see the process that's going on, and not know somewhere in their mind that that person is dying.

BCM: *Do you find it easier when the family is able to talk with the dying person and tell the truth and get things kind of cleared up between them?*

BH: Much easier, because the process that occurs is a process that I think needs to occur in order to facilitate what I think of as a healthy way of dying.

BCM: *I love that phrase* - a healthy way of dying.

BH: I think that it can be that way if they can all come to a point of acceptance. Acceptance and feeling okay about it within yourself. The dying patient can do this by saying, "I am taking care of business that I need to take care of. I've addressed loved ones, family that I need to. I know that I have a disease that has wasted my body and I'm not going to recover from it at this late point, short of a miracle, an unforeseen miracle, and so, okay, now I'm ready." And there are ways the family can certainly facilitate that process.

BCM: *Like. . .?*

BH: I don't mean to think of it all in a negative way, but the ways that I can think of the process working more are things *not* to do. Those can be guideposts for the family. For instance, when the patient is maybe a little bit afraid to talk about death and dying, and yet he knows that he's dying, I often see the family come in and keep saying, "You're going to get better. I'm going to make you comfortable and we are going to get you better and get you up, you'll be eating, you'll be working again." And it's at *that* point where I would just like to say, "That's not really appropriate right now because he's *not* going to get better right now. He needs to talk."

BCM: *I wonder if sometimes the families are doing that for themselves or for the patients?*

BH: As much for themselves as for the patient.

BCM: *So they're still in denial.*

BH: Yes. The charade is probably more for themselves. Because if they really look, they can certainly see what the patient looks like. But they're not prepared to let the patient go yet. They don't want to let go.

BCM: *They're not ready for surrender, acceptance.*

BH: Not at all.

BCM: *And their own fears play a large part in this at times? Is it their own fears, or anger, or grief about the whole situation that blocks acceptance? I have felt these feelings and it has made a difference in my perception of the situation.*

BH: A lot of unresolved issues occur. Some family members say to the very end, "If I had done this differently, or if I had done this, then this whole thing wouldn't be happening."

BCM: *Oh, I know that one very well! It's the whole guilt thing because you are responsible for protecting your child, taking care of your child, making it better, helping them to get over an illness, and when you can't do anything there is a tremendous sense of helplessness.*

BH: You can't really accept that you can't protect them from death.

BCM: *There's a tremendous guilt and rage there.*

BH: And I have heard that over and over again and I've heard mothers in one breath say, "Well, I really know that he's dying," and then turn around fifteen minutes later and go right back to the same line of thinking tied in with the guilt. The tremendous guilt. They'll say to me, "Well, maybe if I had done this differently. And do you think now that if maybe we use this approach, this might help, this might work?" And if I can be comfortable enough with that person then I'll say, "What I really think would work would be for you to sit down and just be yourself, be honest with yourself." But you can't always say that. Sometimes that'll make people very angry. Yet even anger itself is not something I would necessarily shy away from if it were productive. If it would shake something loose.

BCM: *I remember my own family's feelings during Michael's death. We had this enormous rage at death, and often I feel that can be helpful, because in our case it caused us to be honest, to release our feelings. But I can see that sometimes that's not appropriate.*

BH: It's not always appropriate because some people are not ready to listen to their own anger either. Sometimes it just doesn't work.

BCM: *What about when a person is in a coma or in dementia? Do you find it helpful if the family and/or friends can continue to let that person know, "We really love you, we care for you."*

BH: Certainly that can help the quality of the person's ending. Dementia is a little different because there can be so many things going on with dementia. But when it comes to the point of coma, who is to say what a person can hear or not hear? Who is to say what their level of consciousness is aside from what we can just see? Again, for the family as well as for the patient, but certainly for the patient, because I think there's a good possibility that he can hear on some level, I encourage the loving words from the family.

BCM: *One of the things that the Shanti volunteer told us when Michael was in and out of a comatose situation for about ten days was that he was traveling, he was apartment hunting, he was looking for another space to be in and so far he hadn't found anything more beautiful than the place where he was dying. And we could often feel his presence in other parts of the house, even while he was in a coma. And that felt reassuring to us personally because we could see that he was probably in and out, in and out, in and out, so to speak, and then he would go back to where he was, back into that still body.*

BH: I've seen that exact thing you're talking about too. I have seen a patient that I was taking care of who had moved back home, sometimes being in his body and sometimes not, but he always came back "home" to the body. And the serenity when he was "home" was so apparent in the way that he reacted. I can see the analogy of traveling, and needing to come home for that sense of comfort and familiarity.

BCM: *How do you deal with your own feelings? How do you deal with burnout? How do you keep on going year after year?*

BH: I didn't do very well with it when I was first doing what we call aggressive nursing, that is, helping those who are *not* terminally ill to get well. I did go to support groups where I could talk with other people, where I could share my feelings, where I could share the emotions that I was going through. Where I could ask questions to see if other people were sharing and feeling the same thing as I was or if it was just me.

BCM: *And what were some of those emotions that you were feeling?*

BH: Helplessness is the primary emotion. It is very difficult for a caregiver to feel this way. We have been trained to help and to get results by our helping, hopefully, in a very tangible, realistic way.

BCM: *You do this and then this happens. Point A to point B.*

BH: And when we're working with a situation of dying in a hospice type frame of mind, well, the focus is that we *are* going to get the result that we're there for, but the result is death. It can be a very comfortable quality passage through death. And so we *are* attaining it, but again it's very difficult. That's why many physicians have such a difficult time, I think, because their whole focus has been to help people live, not to help people die.

BCM: *Has your focus changed as you've gone on in this work?*

BH: My feelings on death have changed. I certainly no longer have the same focus I did when I first started. Aside from still having a feeling of helplessness, I don't have a focus that I need to do something anymore to make the person live or even to help them die in any particular way. I am very comfortable in helping people to maintain the quality of their lives and to really help them with the dying process. And that's very satisfying to me. If I can help people to be free of pain and deal with emotions that they need to work out, and if I can help the family to deal with their pain and their emotions and watch the whole process come to the concrete terminal point of death, then I get a great deal of satisfaction.

BCM: *Does it help you to learn to deal with your own feeling about death?*

BH: I can't remember a time when I was afraid of death. Maybe my personal beliefs have something to do with that perspective.

BCM: *What are your personal beliefs?*

BH: I was brought up a Catholic. I went to twelve years of school and then I rejected Catholicism. And I rejected religion, overall, and came to the point where I feel even now that the existence that I have here is all there is. It's really difficult for me because I don't concretely believe that you necessarily go any further or do anything after this life.

BCM: *Oh, that's very interesting to hear. Did you believe that before you started this work? Or has this developed since you began working in terminal care situations?*

BH: No, my thoughts haven't changed, I always felt this way.

BCM: *Well I appreciate you being honest. Your thoughts haven't changed? And yet you're still assisting people to make that passage in a loving way.*

BH: That passage. Because in spite of what I'm choosing to believe for myself — I could never say, for instance, that I am an atheist because it's too strong of a statement, just as saying that I'm very religious is too strong of a statement. And I just don't know. That's really where I am. I just don't know. So I try to respect whatever the patient is going through. I *do* know that the majority of patients that I've taken care of do not really claim to have any religious affiliation but certainly are very spiritual people.

BCM: *I love the distinction. Do you think that comes to the fore more because they are dying? Does it, in a sense, force them to look at what they do believe in?*

BH: I think that some of my patients, like myself, tend to put religious affiliation and spirituality away. We don't want to deal with it. But there's something about the process of dying that is so scary or uncertain that people do draw upon that spirituality more than maybe they have for years and years and years. And I certainly am not going to be the one to stand in the way of any process they want to go through. And I would be very resentful of anyone who *did* try to stand in their way.

BCM: *I appreciate that comment. Bill, you talked about your feeling of helplessness. What other feelings are you dealing with here besides helplessness as you go on in this work?*

BH: I certainly feel a great deal of sadness. I've seen people that are brilliant, creative, loving individuals and I don't think it's right that they are going to be taken away from my life. They give so much to others all around them. And then I see people that don't really have these special qualities, and they are healthy. They are thriving. I don't like the injustice of that.

BCM: *So it feels kind of unfair.*

BH: It *is* an unfair feeling and it makes me very sad. It seems like such a crazy loss and one that I certainly can't see any reason for. I don't know what the answer is to that, but that's why sometimes I'll look at somebody who I've been taking care of and I'll just start crying, and I think it's because of the injustice.

BCM: *Well, often it would be a natural release of your emotions. Because there's so much grief. There's so much grief and mourning. Do you go into mourning each time?*

BH: I have to mourn every time.

BCM: *Every time.*

BH: Every individual. That process never stops.

BCM: *What do you do with your anger?*

BH: I used to be hard and keep it all inside me. Actually I used to drink a lot and use a lot of drugs. And that was a way of not dealing with my anger. I decided I didn't want to deal with it, so I thought that if I could just mask it, then it wouldn't bother me. Well, that didn't help me at all. So I stopped that. And I don't drink at all and I don't use drugs at all anymore. And I talk about my feelings. I need to share them with somebody else that can be empathetic and listen. That might be my mother. That might be a close friend that I have, anyone that's close to me, but I need to talk. I cannot keep the feelings unresolved within myself. I think that's the key, that I need to deal with them as openly and honestly as I can. And at least for me, very verbally.

BCM: *Good. What about physical exercise or correct eating, things like that? Does that help?*

BH: Physical exercise is a great issue to bring up. Because at the same time that I stopped drinking and using drugs I started a regimented (for the most part) program of physical exercise as a sort of compensation.

BCM: *Yeah, when you've got time, right?*

BH: When I make myself disciplined enough to do it. And I *am* pretty regimented with it. I seldom miss more than one day a week of exercise. It makes me feel terrific. And it is an excellent way to deal with feelings of anger, sadness, almost any emotions that are jammed up inside. The breathing, the deep breathing that goes along with the exercise process is a large part of it. Whether or not you're even doing an exercise program, you can certainly do deep breathing to release emotional tension.

BCM: *You mentioned talking about your feelings. Do you have a therapy group for caregivers, or is it just that you talk with your colleagues, or do you have a person that you go to privately to help you integrate your feelings about death?*

BH: Well, I have gone to somebody privately, and I have spoken to personal friends. When we set up the home health care agency I manage now, our biggest emphasis, one of our biggest points, was setting up a psychosocial supportive program for the nurses specifically to prevent burnout. We put a tremendous amount of discussion and planning into it, getting input from others on how this might work. We have two psychiatrists working with us, and their whole function is to set up ongoing, sharing seminars for the nurses offered at different times of the month, to fit into the nurse's schedule, but always to be there for the nurses.

BCM: *That's wonderful. You talked also about how for most of us, it is scary to deal with dying on a daily basis, and I found the same thing has happened to me along the way. You almost feel like you're going to catch death because you're around it all the time.*

BH: You're so close to it.

BCM: *So what can you do to get past that point?*

BH: I'm not sure I am past that point yet.

BCM: *What do you do with the fear?*

BH: I'm aware of the fact that it's not going to happen to me. At least not for many years, I hope. So I'm trying to work this out, how I *do* deal with it. Knowing that I'm not going to "catch death," I think that what I do to deal with it better is to watch the process closely, so that I can learn from every individual a little bit more about what they're going through.

BCM: *So it is a mystery.*

BH: It isn't a mystery to me, I've watched death so many times. And I've watched it to the point of the final breath I see. I watch the person's face, I watch what they say, I watch their expressions, I watch their body. And I feel it's like any other subject, the more I can learn about it, the more comfortable I am with it. So I don't run from it. It scares me and...

BCM: *And yet you're faced with it.*

BH: ...and I face it. I look at it and I learn.

BCM: *That's a wonderful, wonderful insight that you are sharing, Bill. There's something that we talked about before, but I'm going to ask the question again to make sure we covered this. Are there any hazards or obstacles that you face when dealing with death and dying? I know we talked about some of the emotions, but are there any other hazards or obstacles which come up that you want to discuss, whether they're practical, professional, or personal?*

BH: If caregivers don't face up to their emotions they go in one of two directions. One of the directions is burnout which we touched on, and that can get to the point of being unhealthy for the caregiver.

I have a great deal of sympathy for the burnout syndrome, because I have experienced it. I have also watched nurses become very calloused in their way of thinking. That's the other end of the spectrum. If they don't deal with the death and dying issue in some healthy way, then they may become so calloused that they can no longer be a caregiver. Those are the two hazards that I very frequently see with nurses. I see them become so hardened they just don't have any more genuine concern with caring for the people they're with. That's the result of not dealing with their own feelings. It's emotional suicide.

BCM: *So that's where the therapies we've been talking about, the nurturing of self, etc., come in?*

BH: Sharing. The sharing and ventilating and exchanging ideas.

BCM: *Do you ever get to the point where there's so much exhaustion, you just need to take a month or a year off?*

BH: Yes, that happens sometimes. I took time off when I left my last position because I wasn't dealing effectively with my burnout, and I did take two months off just to be away from it all. And I've watched numerous other nurses and caregivers do this. It is a big issue. Nurses have come up to me and said, "Well, Bill, you're giving us two weeks a year vacation, but if I've been with a patient that has just died, and I've been with that person for three or four months, I need some time away and maybe that's going to be a month or two. How are you going to compensate me for that time?" And I thought about it and now I say, "Whatever technical policies we need to follow, whether it's giving you a leave of absence or some other arrangement, we will do it. You need your time and you are going to get your time." There's really no debating the necessity of that. So we do that for our nurses because we have all been through it ourselves.

BCM: *That's wonderful. In a sense, then, even in the face of AIDS, this horrible crisis, a new model of health care is emerging. More and more people are choosing to die at home, whatever their terminal illness is. Caregivers are learning to take care of themselves professionally and to change the structure of the nursing world.*

BH: We need to do that because the AIDS epidemic certainly is not going to go away within the next four or five years. And it's going to increase probably tenfold in the number of cases we're going to see. And as you say, more and more people, *whatever* the nature of their illness, are choosing to die at home. If we don't have caregivers to take care of the patients, then the whole commitment that I chose four years ago is defeated. My emphasis for that very reason is to focus as much on the health of the caregiver as on the quality of life of the patient.

BCM: *What you're saying is very, very important. The healthier the caregiver, whether a professional nurse or a concerned loved one, the better able they are to take care of an ill person.*

BH: Right. Also, I have so often seen that when somebody loves somebody so much who's dying, they can no longer see the forest for the trees and they want to do *everything* that person needs. And so many times I've sat down and said, "You are loving so much, you're so close, that you're not going to be able to help at all if you can't step back and give yourself some time and let somebody else share some of the responsibility." And so the emotional and physical health of the caregiver, regardless of who that caregiver is, needs to be addressed. I spoke only last week with a man who was just not able to provide nursing care for his loved one. I told him to look into some other viable alternatives and to look at how he was handling his loved one's death right now. Because the patient involved was not going to die immediately. I told this man, the caregiver, "You are not going to survive at the pace you're going much longer. You need to recognize that fact and deal with it. I would like to come and sit with you and we'll talk about this and we'll work out what you can do to be healthy to yourself."

BCM: *Healthy to yourself, yes.*

BH: So that you can be loving and caring and giving to your friends, to your patients, to your loved one, and to your family. If that person can't learn to be healthy for themselves, then their whole purpose is going to be sabotaged. Their plan is not going to work.

BCM: *And some of us become very dysfunctional, either when we're dealing with the death of someone we love or afterward. It's almost like you hold on until they are gone and then you collapse and fall apart. And it takes a while to pick up the pieces and get back together. Do you have any guidelines for grief recovery? I'm hearing that there are different mourning periods. First they were saying, ''If you lose someone you need at least a year to grieve.'' And what I'm seeing is well-meaning friends telling you to buck up a week after this has happened. They say, ''You know, don't you, that the person you loved is now happy and at peace.'' When what you need is the comfort. And now I'm seeing that people are saying it could be two years, it could be five years, it could be six years or more. Are you seeing that also with the caregivers?*

BH: It's really on a very individual basis, but I speak with caregivers, nurses themselves even, who are still talking and going through the grieving and mourning process on a patient that they had taken care of two years ago. I can tell by the feelings and emotions that they're still expressing, that in no way has that process been completed yet.

BCM: *Do you have any ideas or suggestions on how the grieving process can be completed?*

BH: I think again that the best suggestion I have is to face the issue, recognize the feelings. You can't always understand your feelings, but if you don't ignore them or deny them away, then you begin the healing process right at that point.

BCM: *Much better than to resist the feelings.*

BH: Know that this person has gone on. That that passage is now complete and we will not see him breathe, or talk, or move anymore. Professional caregivers can help the grieving to acknowledge the death just by acknowledging it themselves.

BCM: *It's a reality check, in a sense.*

BH: You can't begin dealing with the emotions that surface if you haven't really dealt with the reality of the death. This is why some sort of celebration of life or some kind of funeral service or memorial service or whatever you would like to call it, and however you want to treat it, is so important. It's a way to not only have a chance to say goodbye, in a way that's important to you and to the person you loved, but also to begin your own healing process very effectively, allowing the mourning and the grieving.

BCM: *Do you have anything else that you really would like to share that could help caregivers and families?*

BH: The most important advice that I think I could give is to learn from every situation that you have an opportunity to be exposed to. Learn so that you continue to grow with yourself and so that you can help other people to be comfortable with whatever process they need to go through. Don't shy away from experiences, emotions, situations. Don't deny them. Don't pretend they're not happening. Don't pretend that you're above them or that they don't mean anything.

BCM: *Are you a very different person than you were when you first started with this work?*

BH: I'm a little wiser person, I think. I don't believe I'm different in the level of caring or loving than when I started. I think I'm better able now to help other people to go through the passage of dying and death. And to help the family or the friends around them also go through that passage. I'm better equipped to do that emotionally, while didactically there are some skills that I've learned. But my level of loving and caring is the same now as it was four years ago.

BCM: *What about the future of how we take care of people in our society who are dying? Is there a model that you would like to see? Some things that you would like to see changed? Legally, politically, medically, humanely?*

BH: I would certainly like to see the trend move more towards allowing the individual to make their own decisions on what to do with their life or death process. I would tend to go towards a loving euthanasia.

BCM: *Euthanasia. I have trouble with that word. Some people are calling it other things now.*

BH: I do tend to go very much towards that philosophy. I believe that we have the right to decide what we want to do with our bodies and how we want to leave them. And so, looking from a political or a moral or a legal point of view, I simply would like to see this right to decide becoming more acceptable. I would also certainly like to see much more in helping the dying to be in a home environment that's comfortable. One that's not rigid with regulations and policies that institutions by their very nature almost need to follow. I would like to see a person have a sweeter, more satisfying transition from life to death. I certainly would like to see that!

BCM: *Less traumatic and more loving and less in isolation?*

BH: Yes, exactly. I think that's what we're all striving for. Like the Dying Person's Bill of Rights.

BCM: *Yes. It's so beautiful. And it says it all.*

The Gift
of
Healing

THE FREEING FORCE

Release.
Do not cease
To be joyful, the free.
To be the best that you can be.

Release.
You will find surcease
in a free-floating peace.
Release, release.

Flow.
Go within. Go
To the holy center. Go.

You are your own mentor.
You are your own soul's source.

Rejoice.
Faith is the freeing force.
Rejoice.
Rejoice.

— BETTYCLARE MOFFATT

4

Jim Geary is Executive Director of Shanti Project, San Francisco. His article is reprinted here with permission from *AIDS: A Self-Care Manual*.

Experiencing the Power of Healing

This evening I would like to share with you a few words about healing, grieving, and overcoming barriers. In 1982, a friend and colleague of mine who was dying talked to me about healing. Paul was a father and a psychologist. He had tried many traditional as well as alternative forms of treatment, from interferon and chemotherapy, to a macrobiotic diet and visualization work.

I encountered Paul just before he was to leave for the Philippines to work with what he called a psychic surgeon. It seemed to many of us who knew Paul that he might not return alive.

I told him that, in my opinion, he had more faith in his ability to manifest recovery than all of us helpers at the Shanti Project put together. Paul smiled and shared with me how he had accepted that he didn't know what the actual outcome would be regarding his ongoing effort to bring about physical healing. He also said he realized that he might die, but he approached his life with an attitude that "anything is possible." He was living each precious moment to its maximum.

Paul taught me how to look at healing differently: to understand that healing isn't necessarily an end result, but a moment-to-moment way of living that empowers one to be and understand more who one is. Healing can be both accepting and/or challenging what we call fate. Healing is a way of living in which we give definition to ourselves through the eyes of others. Healing can occur through both metaphysical and/or practical thinking.

In my weekly support group members sometimes get seemingly polarized around the issues of healing and its relationship to attitude. For example, a person using a metaphysical approach, that is, mind over matter, in working with his illness, may determine that a person who talks about dying, or who is feeling depressed about his condition, is in fact giving power to that condition, thus enhancing the possibility of death as a likely outcome. Conversely, a person who is dealing directly with issues surrounding dying and depression may determine that the metaphysical thinker is denying his or her true feelings and is afraid to look at the possibility of dying.

Each of these points of view has merit and something to offer the other. The metaphysical thinker is correct in pointing out that what we focus on does, to a large degree, become our reality; yet it is also a metaphysical principle that what one resists, persists. Dealing with one's fears of dying and feelings of depression can be disempowering or empowering. Often it is only by becoming deeper in touch with our feelings of disempowerment and helplessness that we tap into a larger source of personal power.

Healing is, regardless of the success of the outcome as viewed by others, the inner knowledge of our own ability to deal with what we are experiencing. It is our ability to open to each changing moment and see ourselves anew.

My friend Paul died healing. Healing himself and others of our narrowness of vision. Healing us of our apathetic compliance with what we temporarily perceive as inevitable. How seemingly difficult it is for us to open to that eternal process of becoming more. For us to begin to see miracles not as otherworldly, but as self-worthy and attainable.

Dave, a friend of mine who is ill, told me recently of an image he had in which he saw an enormous door. As he approached and opened the door, he was flooded with the most intense light he had ever seen. As he passed through the door into the light, feelings of health, joy, and inner brilliance filled him. In this real moment of Dave's life, Dave was shown a way for him and for us. How seldom do we similarly allow ourselves to enter that light and shine, to feel joy and celebrate our physical and mental well-being?

As people who are dying explore healing, they expand the perceived limits of our human condition. As helpers to the dying, we may need to recognize that the people for whom we do service may be more deeply in touch with their own transformative powers than we are with ours. Hopefully, if this does occur, our reaction will not be one of having failed them but a reaction of awe and gratitude for our increased awareness of our own capabilities.

When we stop focusing only on the external outcome of healing, and pause more often to recognize and surpass our fears and our judgments that limit and belittle us, we will see healing as possible in each moment in our lives, thereby knowing to a greater degree our inner magnificence and brilliance. It is so essential that we continue to feel.

So many people fear that getting too involved leads

to burnout. It is my experience that it is *not* getting involved that leads to feelings of anxiousness, of being overwhelmed, and of eventual burnout. It is through stuffing our feelings of grief, anger, and helplessness that we will fill ourselves with stress, internalized rage, and weariness, not to mention ulcers. Change in any form is hard; the dying of one's lover, child, friend is hellish. We must remember that feeling powerful emotions is not negative thinking. You may need to scream for what seems like forever, or cry till your heart feels like it is being stabbed with each incoming breath. But scream and cry we must if we are ever to feel whole again.

We must also find ways to help others in their grief, remembering that this is sometimes as simple as listening to the anguish in a father's heart, stemming from a wish that he had told his daughter or son how much he loved them.

Let us remember that in opening to current grief issues we often tap a well of unresolved issues of grief collected over a lifetime; grief for friends and family members who perhaps died years ago; grief past or present.

It is so easy to compare our grief circumstances with others' as a way of invalidating our own. It is essential that regardless of the circumstances leading to our grief, we take the time and the loving self-nurturance to heal those wounded parts of ourselves. Each of us must first find our own way to accept grieving and dying as a part of living. For it is ultimately only by accepting the changing nature of life that we are able to release the past and find meaning and new courage in the moment.

For me, it is also a question of how I want to live my life. At times, it feels easier to live halfway; to shy away from strangers; to reason that I am already doing enough; to allow my own sense of inadequacy to gain the upper hand. But I know this isn't the way I want to live my life.

My dear friend Pete is dying of pneumocystis pneumonia. Pete was different from many people dealing with life-threatening illness in that he always wanted to talk about how *I* was doing. In many ways, with Pete I had found the best friend I had never before had time for. Although only in his early thirties, Pete possessed a grandfather-like wisdom and gentleness in which I found much comfort. Recently my friend had his third bout of pneumonia and was placed on large doses of morphine. The Pete I knew and loved disappeared. He became withdrawn, self-absorbed, lingering.

Despite all my years of counseling the ill, I felt entirely inadequate in how to be there for my friend. I so much wanted him to die, as much for me as for him, so I wouldn't have to feel such pain. As Pete withdrew, I withdrew. Each visit with him was awkward and uncomfortable. Finally I realized that part of the reason I was feeling so badly was that I had let the most important quality of our relationship die before Pete did. The quality of honesty to tell Pete what I was feeling. The next time I was with him I told him how I missed my buddy and that a big part of me was hoping he would die. To my surprise and relief, when I told Pete these things, he said he understood. He said that he, too, was tired of lingering, of trying to show interest in the lives of others, and of having to say repeated goodbyes.

In that moment I found myself and my best friend again because as difficult as it was, I risked being real. I want to seize each moment, to keep my heart open, to make eye contact, to risk being authentic even if it is painful. I know that living life this way will bring us closer to ourselves and each other. And in living life in this manner, we will have to look at and continue to work on our old tapes of racism, sexism, and perhaps the worst of all, "selfism." That is the belief that we as individuals are guilty, unworthy, incapable, powerless, less or better than our brothers and sisters.

I asked one of our board members, Gary, several months before he died what he had learned throughout his illness.

Gary responded, "Love really is the answer." Gary wasn't sure what the question was, but he was sure that as simple as it sounded, love was the solution. Gary staked his life on that solution.

*   *   *

Bobby Reynolds led the following meditation for the 500 participants at the Fourth National AIDS Forum. Bobby was a board member of Shanti Project, San Francisco, and co-chair of the National Association of People With AIDS/ARC. Bobby died April 27, 1987. This healing meditation is reprinted by permission from *AIDS: A Self-Care Manual*.

A Healing Meditation

Please close your eyes, sit comfortably, and begin breathing deeply.

Become aware of the heart beating in your chest. Notice that your heartbeat is calm and regular. I would like you to imagine that the place in your chest where you feel your heart beating is the part of your being that is the most loving. As you take your next breath, imagine that this heartspace is being filled with a warm golden light ... a light of love. You can feel your heart pump this healing light to every part of your body. It touches that part of you which feels pain and grief, which feels anger and hurt, which feels fear and sorrow. As this light continues to radiate within you, you are calmed and nurtured and comforted. As it permeates every cell of your body, you are able to realize your own special uniqueness and how truly worthy of love you are. This love within you continues to grow and becomes stronger with every breath. It reaches outside of your body and merges with the love of the sisters and brothers around you.

The power of this love is mighty. In this moment, in this room, our love is the most powerful energy in the universe. And, we can form this energy into a beam of lovelight. With this beam, we can reach out to the fear, hate, and hysteria that surrounds us. We can educate, we can become leaders and role models for the world. We can send this lovelight within ourselves to touch the doubts and anxieties that may torment us. We can use this lovelight to find the strength to face another day, the courage to continue taking risks.

We can help all segments of our society to unite with a common purpose, a very human purpose, to overcome AIDS. We can reach out to those people with AIDS in the small towns and the big cities throughout our country and beyond. We can send them our wishes for healing and well-being. We can give them the strength and courage to stand tall and speak out for their rights.

We can send this powerful beam of lovelight to the hearts and consciousness of the policy makers in all levels of government and business, and we can believe in this moment in our ability to affect change.

And we can effect changes in those we meet in our everyday life. Take a moment now and picture in your mind and heart all those people with AIDS who have touched your life. Look deeply into their eyes, see the part of them that is a playful child, that is vulnerable and needs nurturing. See the Godself, Buddha, the wise woman or wise man. See the part of them that is a survivor. If they have died, picture them sitting next to you, holding your hand. Remember the memories you have woven together, the history of your friendship. Take this opportunity to tell them again that you love them, or you may want to say goodbye or to give them another message.

Their image slowly begins to fade and gradually transforms into ribbons of colors dancing in the wind; they continue to dance in your heart for all time. Know that we can surround our friends wherever they may be with our love, which is a healing force that knows no limitations. We can cry together over the pain of our losses. We can scream together our rage over the unfairness. Together, we can share the joy of rainbows, sunsets, the warm glow of a smile. Together, we can share ourselves fully. By not holding back, we become vulnerable. By being vulnerable, we can allow ourselves to heal and be healed, to care and be cared for, to love and be loved. By reaching out to another person to touch another life with compassion and love, we can work miracles.

Take another breath, hold it, and release it slowly.

Know that when you feel low or when those doubts and anxieties arise, you have a place to go, a place deep within yourself that is safe and nurturing and loving. AIDS has disrupted many lives. It has left us with much heartache and with many questions unanswered. But know, in every cell of your being, that your loving, your caring, your just *being* there, does make a difference and will continue to be a help to those of us living with AIDS.

Take a deep breath, hold it, and release it slowly.

Slowly, begin to come back to this room. Become aware of the people around you. Feel your feet on the floor. Together, we can face the rough times and we can celebrate the good times. Together we can meet the challenges of this epidemic. Together— for we are a family and we are not alone. Slowly open your eyes and look around you at all these wonderful people.

Bobby Reynolds concluded the meditation with a special request that everyone join him in a song that had been a favorite of his for many years. Recently, it had taken on a new meaning to him and to the people close to him. The song is "Somewhere Over the Rainbow."

The Gift
of
Understanding

Be patient towards all that is unanswered in your heart
and try to love the questions themselves.

Do not seek answers
that cannot be given to you,
because you would not be able to live them.

And the point is to live everything.

Live the questions now,
perhaps you will gradually,
without noticing it,
live along some distant day
into the answers.

— RANIER MARIA RILKE

5

Laurie Williams, a home health care nurse who works with terminally ill patients, took care of David Kessler's father, Joey Shea, for the last few weeks of his life. *(See The Gift of Adventure for Joey's story. -ed.)* I interviewed Laurie and David a few days before Joey died.

David is one of the most loving young men I have ever met. A male nurse who saw a need and opened himself up to fill that need, he started the first home health care agency for AIDS patients in Los Angeles county, Progressive Nursing Services.

As Laurie and David and I talked, I became aware of what a remarkable opportunity it was to hear their deepest feelings about the whole range of caregiver issues. Their insights helped me, as I know they will help you, to understand the caregivers who work with the dying; their grief, their burnout, their coping strategies. We talked also about our ideal visions for the future for caregivers and for the dying.

BCM: *Well, mostly I want to know how this tour of duty differs from other people that you have taken care of who have gone through the dying process.*

LW: Well, in this job it's kind of a pleasure for me because Joey's eighty-three years old, it's natural, you know, and he is so accepting of it, or at least it appears as though he's very accepting of death and that he's ready to go. And of course I should note that I usually take care of AIDS patients that are young men; it's not time for them. And they fight and they struggle and you do try to help them through the process of dying. It's devastating because you don't know what to do, you don't know how to help them get through it so that they can start coming to terms with dying, and help the people they love that are there, help *them* get through it, too.

BCM: *Yes. It seems like such a tragedy when it's a young person.*

LW: It's terrible. It's terrible.

BCM: *And when it's an older person, it's like this beautiful gentleman says, it's the next step.*

LW: It is, it's the natural turn of events. We know when we're born we are destined to die. But you're not destined to die at twenty-five, twenty-six, twenty-seven, twenty-eight.

BCM: *There's such a sense of unfinished business.*

LW: There is.

BCM: *And almost a sense of being robbed of your life.*

LW: They *are* robbed. And they suffer terribly. And I've noticed with AIDS patients that there is such a high level of stress that they can't sleep, they're afraid to sleep, they're afraid not to sleep, there's a lot of disorientation. And I don't know how to help. I don't know how to get to them so that I can put them at peace. So that they can rest. So that they can come to terms with dying. Because they're in such denial, they're not open to what you have to say when you try to tell them that if they rest things will be better in the morning, that their minds are just kind of stretched out and tired. I've really noticed that in them. Just a constant exhaustion. They fight. They struggle.

BCM: *Yes. Bill Hodgson, another nurse who deals with AIDS patients, told me that his first case was a young man, and he kept trying to make him comfortable, but the patient sat on the edge of the bed all night long, because he was so afraid that if he went to sleep he would die. And the stress that Bill went through! Then of course, with Michael, my son who died of AIDS, what we went through was the most transfiguring experience and at the same time it was the most devastating experience, year after year and week after week and month after month, to move from emotion to emotion, from experience to experience.*

LW: And to watch them waste away.

BCM: *Yes, and to move from the struggle to the acceptance. And I wondered if the nurses go through all of that range of emotions, of the rage and the terror and the guilt and the grief.*

LW: I seem to attach to my patients very quickly. Because I have children. (Laughter).

BCM: *So do I. I say, "Thank you God" every day for all of my children still living.*

LW: Oh, that's what I say. "Thank you God that my child doesn't have AIDS." So when I go in there I have a pretty motherly attitude toward them, because I think, "Gee, this could be my kid." And so I strive when I take care of them to treat them the way I would want my son treated. I respect everything that they are going through. Anything they want I do it, whatever they want. And so I do go through a lot of things with them because I just attach. And when they die I have a real hard time of it. I don't want to go through it again for awhile. I just had a patient who died before I came on this case and I said, "Oh, thank God," because I don't feel the same when I'm here with Joey Shea as I do when I'm taking care of the young ones. I mean, I don't feel uncomfortable here with him dying. It feels just right.

BCM: *He's made it right.*

LW: Yes. He's made it right.

BCM: *But when you have patient after patient, the young ones that you've had that are dying of AIDS or other terminal diseases, what do you do afterwards to get yourself to the point where you can go into the next situation again and take care of someone who is terminally ill?*

LW: Well, immediately I go home and I cry.

BCM: *There's a lot of that going around. (Laughter). This last couple of years.*

LW: I immediately go home and cry and fortunately for me, I've only had two patients die while I've been there. When they die and you're not there it's not as bad as when they die and you *are* there, because you're more separated from the situation. So both of the times that I've had a patient die, I've gone home and I've been fortunate because my boyfriend is there, so I just collapse in his arms and he just hugs me and pampers me and babies me and then I mourn.

After this last one died, I just said, "Okay, today is a day of mourning." And that's what we do at the house. Everybody pampers me and babies me and it's a day of mourning.

BCM: *Doesn't it take longer than a day, though?*

LW: Yes, it does. And then what I do is I don't work with dying patients for a while. I go back into the hospital. I work in the hospital, which is not the greatest environment, but at least it's not all death and dying, it's people that are going to get better, people that are going to go home. There's hope. So I do that. Yes, it does take a long time to grieve. And this last one, this young man who died, when I think about him I am still in mourning. It's been a week.

BCM: *Just a week and you're already taking a new case.*

LW: No, this is different.

BCM: *This is a beautiful case.*

LW: Yes.

BCM: *Have your ideas on dying and on nursing, on taking care of terminally ill patients, have they changed over the years as you have experienced this?*

LW: I haven't been doing this that long, but my ideas on death and dying have changed considerably. I was talking to David last night about how it puts you more in touch with your own mortality. Yes, you are going to die and everyone is going to die. I think it's given me a healthier approach to life and to death. And I think that since I have gone through this a few times and seen these patients die, it's really made me a better nurse. It gives me more insight into other people's lives. It makes me a more caring person. I think that death and dying has done a lot for me.

BCM: *I felt sometimes like my heart was being ripped open and it would never be closed because there was no veil anymore between me and other people. And I'm wondering, when you go out into the "real world" or the "ordinary world," do you have difficulty with people being superficial? Do you have difficulty dealing with all the trivial things that go on elsewhere when you are dealing at such an intimate, intense level with people all the time?*

LW: You mean when I'm away from nursing?

BCM: *Yeah. I'm just wondering. That's just one of my things I'm dealing with.*

LW: I just hate to tell you this, but I just don't get out and mingle amongst them. (Laughter).

BCM: *Good for you. You talked about how your views had changed on death and dying. Do you fear death?*

LW: Umm, not as much as I used to, which is interesting. You know, you'd think that after being around it for a while you'd fear it a little bit more. But no, I don't. I fear it less than I did before. You know after they die, they're so peaceful. Aren't they? They are so peaceful. And it's just like something has happened that has made them that peaceful, that the struggle is finally over. Even the worst strugglers are peaceful.

BCM: *What about your own struggle with life? Are you less of a struggler now that you have been with patients who have died?*

LW: Am I struggling with life itself or denying death? I probably do struggle less than I did. When these things happen, I feel like I need to find something in every day of my life to enjoy and I need to bring myself more pleasure, that I need to do more things for myself. That's another thing I'm getting out of it. I mean, I went into nursing because I am a caregiver, but I found out that I need to get something back. So I'm more demanding. I notice that in my own house I'm now demanding that my family give me more. I've always done everything in the house. You know, I go out and work twelve hours and I go home and it's still okay for me to cook and clean and do all the stuff that I've always done when I didn't work twelve hours. Well I've found out now that people need to give back to me what I give to them. I deserve it. And they've started doing those things. My kids, I mean.

BCM: *So it's more of a balance. You have to fill up so that you will have something to give the next time.*

LW: It *is* more of a balance. And they've started doing more. Not that they do the laundry, but I've gotten them to pick up the laundry, to put the laundry in its proper place, which is a big thing. And you know, it's really interesting how everybody has kind of pitched in.

DK: And you know one thing that Laurie said earlier that makes her case very fortunate is that so many times nurses experience this type of grief and then go home to their family and friends, where they're met with, "Well you're a nurse, don't you know how to deal with death? I mean, isn't death a part of your work? What's the big deal?" Or, "Oh, I thought you were supposed to maintain a professional distance. Aren't you goofing up here?"

BCM: *These are important issues that you mention, David, and I do want to elicite specifically anything and everything that you do for your own mourning process, your own recovery process. And that could be both the practical and the esoteric ways that you deal with all this. Being in the world in a very special certain way, dealing with death and dying, and then going back to people who just don't know.*

LW: You know, it's kind of interesting. I think that one of the things that happens as part of the dying process is that people feed off of you and you feed off of them. You know, you gain strength from them and they gain strength from you. And they give you the courage to go on. There was so much appreciation from my last patient, from his friend, and from his family. His mother and father came, and they gave me so much back. And it seems like you're not giving as much as you're getting back. I even feel like that here. I feel like I'm getting a lot from Joey. And I don't know how much he's getting from me and I do make him happy, but...

DK: Don't sell yourself short. He loves you.

LW: I know he does, David. And I love him.

BCM: *I appreciate your being so frank because these are valuable insights that we all need to know.*

LW: But I do get a lot from them. Then when they die, and you leave when they die, well, you know how it feels when somebody dies. You feel terrible. You go into mourning and that's another thing. People don't know how to mourn. No one has ever been taught how to mourn. It's a very personal, very private thing.

BCM: *You can't do it wrong.*

LW: You can't do it wrong. Thank God.

DK: Paradise into reality is people who mourn well.

BCM: *Yes. One week after my son died, the tears were coming, I couldn't hold them back, and people would say, "What's the matter with you? Don't you know he's happy and at peace? Get on with your life." One week! And my rage would come up. How dare they negate these feelings I'm going through?*

LW: But I think there's another thing that happens sometimes when a loved one dies. You have this other reaction where you may say to yourself, "Oh my God, it's only a week and I'm stopping mourning. This can't be right." But yet, the person who has died doesn't want you to mourn. And they'll tell you that.

BCM: *It's your recovery process. It is your recovery process.*

LW: Here is a person who has fought and struggled till the last breath has been drawn, to live, and when we go into such terrible mourning, we're not *living*. We're not doing what they wanted us to do.

BCM: *The loss is for us. It's not a loss for them. When Michael died, I called my mother and she said, "Thank God, he's at peace." In the midst of our sorrow we were rejoicing because we loved him so much and we didn't want to see him suffer in that deteriorating body week after week. But oh, the mourning! At first there was peace and relief. But then, when you realize that the person you love isn't going to be around for you, and I'm talking about this young person . . .*

LW: See, yeah, but it's different as a parent.

BCM: *You need to take a very long time to go through healing the part of you that has experienced that devastating loss because it is such a loss.*

LW: It's worse for a family member. As a mother, it's so sad. I had a baby that died at birth, so I know what it feels like to lose somebody you love. And some people say, "Well, you never knew the baby." And that's just not true, that's not the way it is.

BCM: *It's a part of you.*

LW: It is, and you suffer. And it's an unnatural turn of events to have your children die before you.

BCM: *It violates the order of the universe.*

LW: It does. That it definitely does. It is unnatural. It's more natural for your father to die. That is a natural turn of events, especially at your age and at his age. But not for *you* to die.

DK: Right. Absolutely.

LW: If the positions were reversed, if it were you in that bed and your father was taking care of you, I don't think we would be having these conversations.

DK: Exactly.

LW: Because there would be so much pain. I'm just saying from personal experience, no matter how "spiritually aware" you believe you are, there is such rage at your child being taken from you. Someone that is a part of you being ripped up like a tree, a young tree. And I think that colors a lot of what is going on. That you're helpless to protect your child.

BCM: *Oh yes! But David and I were talking about how when his father goes, it's the last person in the world left ahead of him in his life. You're all alone and you're a grown up now, David. In fact, there's nobody between you and death or between you and the rest of the world.*

DK: Yes, and somehow there's an inner peace that it *is* supposed to be that way. That is the order of the universe. I've prepared for this my whole life. We *do* think that some day we will lose our parents. We *don't* think, "Someday I'll be burying my children."

BCM: *No, we don't.*

DK: And the other thing about mourning is that I believe that mourning is something that should be shared. Share that point in yourself that's grieving. It's so wonderful to be able to do that because you know that there will be a time that allows the mourning process to subside. There will be a part of your heart that will mourn forever and yet you will not grieve forever.

BCM: *I think it's wonderful that we are sharing this now with each other because death itself has been such a taboo subject in our world, in the Western world.*

LW: Well, it's like it's not natural.

BCM: *It's amazing to me that caregivers beginning in this type of work can move through their own conscious and unconscious fears of death. To me, that seems to be the great lesson and I wondered if you would like to comment on that.*

LW: Well, I wanted to say something about the way I feel about the mourning process with regards to mourning people who are relative strangers, although they aren't by the time they die, even if it's only a couple of weeks that you're taking care of them. You know everything about them by that time. But it's not as bad as a real close friend or a family member or a lover dying. Because then you *really* know them, and you've experienced life's joys with them and you're going to miss them. Whereas as a nurse you haven't experienced life's joys with them, you've only experienced life's trials and pain with them.

BCM: *That's a really good insight. I hadn't thought of that before.*

LW: You usually haven't seen joy in that person. You've just seen them miserable. Although, through this old guy out here, I experience some of life's joys with him.

BCM: *As I was coming over here a part of me was thinking, "This is the most wonderful opportunity to meet with David's father and to share with both of them," and another part of me was really dreading this today. I* thought, "Oh, we're going to bring back all of my grief for Michael." And instead I feel so invigorated because of the joy that is in the room!

LW: That is the way I feel. And I mean I'm sorry for you, David, but when I come here I feel *good* about being here.

DK: Oh, *I* feel good about you being here too!

LW: Whether he's dying or not dying, you know.

DK: Well isn't that the key for us, to feel good whether or not he's dying?

LW: Yes.

DK: You know, that night in intensive care, it was almost like he made a miraculous recovery that night. It's almost like the more we accepted death, the more I embraced life. The more we don't run from death, the more we learn.

BCM: *That's very profound, David.*

DK: You mentioned the idea about death being a taboo. This is on the market now. (Picks up a copy of a large book called *A Complete Guide for Patients and Their Families*). It's one of the books in home and health care. It has everything in it. Every type of patient, every illness. Just everything. Anything you want to know about home health care is in this book. If you look up in the index under "death," you know what you'll find?

BCM: *What?*

DK: Nothing! They didn't mention it.

BCM: *You're kidding.*

DK: This is our society.

BCM: *David, what did you learn in school about death?*

DK: Laurie and I went to school together actually.

LW: Yes, we did.

BCM: *What did you learn about death there?*

LW: We didn't learn anything.

DK: We didn't learn a thing.

LW: Not one thing. I never remember anybody ever talking to us about death, David.

DK: I know.

LW: It was just something that we did not talk about. You know when I started doing this, I said, "Oh my God, what do I do when somebody dies? How do I know what to do? How do I handle it? What do I do?" And I just sort of went in and the first patient I had, he was forty, and you know, it was a real comfortable situation for me because he was close to my age and I felt like I could sit and talk to him. Yet, when I got to his house, I said, "Oh my God, what am I going to do here? How am I going to handle all this?" Because I was so unprepared for it. And all we had learned in school was that you're supposed to help people through the dying process.

BCM: *How?*

LW: *How.* Exactly. *How* do you do it? Well, in a way it wasn't so bad that they didn't try to teach us in school how to handle death and dying because, as a nurse, I do everything by rote. If I don't have it memorized then I don't know how to do it.

BCM: *You've got to memorize death, is that it? (Laughter).*

LW: So, remembering my first time, I went in this house and I thought, "Oh my God, what do I do?" It was my first day. And I think it's always the same the first day, things are a little tense, everybody is testing everybody else, you're not real comfortable, you want to do it right because everybody's there watching you and you think,

"Oh my God if I trip over this chair one more time they're going to throw me out of here because I'm a klutz." So you know, you kind of go through *that* when you go in. Well, as I was there longer and longer, this man and I developed a wonderful relationship. And I thought, "This is what it is. This is why they didn't teach us this in school, because it's an experience that you have to *experience*. Everytime I go someplace now, I wait to see what the patient is going to do. And I follow their lead. I am just being myself, but I see what *they* want to talk about. In school they told us, "Yeah, get them in there to talk about death." Well they don't all want to talk about death. Sometimes they want to review their lives. Sometimes they *don't* want to review their lives.

BCM: *Sometimes they just want to be taken care of.*

LW: Sometimes they just want to be taken care of. That's right. And some of them want to be children again. And so that's what I do now. I just see what they want to do. What they want to talk about.

BCM: *David, what was your first experience with a dying patient like? How did you move from being a male nurse in a hospital setting to being an advocate of home health care and doing the hospice nursing?*

DK: Well, the way it actually worked is that there's what's called Registries in Town, temporary nursing services, where nurses work one or two days a week just to supplement their income. Back in '81, '82, '83, I was doing that. And one day one of the services called me and said, "We have one of those AIDS patients and we cannot get any nurses to go out and we know that this isn't going to be something you'll want to do but

would you at least try it?" And it was amazing
that in my mind I thought, "What are they talking about? Why *wouldn't* I do that?" So I went on
this particular case and I thought it was going to
be for just two days, and it turned out to be nine
months.

BCM: *Nine months.*

DK: And I was amazed with this man that I met. I first
walked in back in those days, with the mask on
and the gloves on and all covered up. I laugh to
myself now because I thought not only am I pro-
tected from AIDS but if there had been a nuclear
fallout I probably would have lived (laughter). So
I walked into the man's room and I just talked to
him with all this stuff on. I asked him "What
must this be like for you to have me here with all
this on?" And he said to me with tears in his
eyes, "The hardest part is, I know no one will
ever dance with me again."

BCM: *How beautiful.*

DK: And obviously it wasn't long after that before I
took my garb off. And I made sure that before he
died we danced.

BCM: *That's a beautiful story.*

DK: Absolutely. And then what happened from there
is, all of a sudden I became known as one of
those nurses that would go out on these cases. So
I was in such high demand and there were a
group of us that would end up on all the AIDS
cases at home, most all the dying cases at home.
And we felt like we weren't getting supported by
the nursing services. You know, they didn't really
care what was going on. They didn't feel for this
patient. They were just big corporations from
back east. So when I thought of starting Progres-

sive Nursing Services, I really thought it was just going to be a small association of nurses that was gonna just help these few patients around here. I had no idea that this disease would turn into what it's turned into. So that was my first case and that's basically how my work with the terminally ill developed.

BCM: *When I talk with caregivers I find that everyone I meet, well, you all have such a different attitude from the general attitude. It's almost like there's the civilians and then there are the people who are in the know about what is really going on.*

DK: And the two shall never communicate.

BCM: *It's as if people in our society think that dealing with dying is dangerous. As if it were contagious.*

LW: Yeah.

BCM: *And they feel like if they don't think about it, it will go away. Yet I'm always so amazed at the beautiful life processes that I see happening when people* do *accept death.*

DK: Yeah. My life is more full and I'm more clear and more happier than I've ever been.

LW: Me too.

BCM: *Me too. Three.*

DK: And as much as I hate loss, and I mean, I'm sure since I have such an issue with loss that it's no accident of the universe that I have a nursing service. But as much as there is loss, there's as much that I get. Sometimes when I do sit by these people's bedsides, I am in awe and I think *I'm* the student, *they* are the teacher. And let me just hear what they have to say. The things you learn are incredible. And realistically, you know that the teachers and nurses could have never taught it to you.

LW: No, they could never have taught it. And it's always the same thing in nursing school. You would have had to memorize it, anyway. If you didn't do it right it was wrong.

DK: Right. (Laughter).

BCM: *Even though it is the most profound experience that you have ever gone through and the work that goes on is so intense, what do you do the rest of the time when you are not taking care of a patient? Laurie talked about mourning and of being taken care of by people in her family. Do you have anything else that you'd like to tell us?*

DK: Well, I think the most important thing is what she said. Just realize that it's all a part of the experience and all of this professional distance stuff that we hear is just garbage. Realize that you *are* a human being and thank God human beings feel! And you're entitled to have those feelings and to make time for them. The other thing I want to mention is about seeing people dying time after time, the constant crisis. The problem is so big that you can give twenty-four hours of yourself and you still won't make a dent in the AIDS crisis, or in any terminally ill situation. So the reality is that you have to know what you can give and see yourself in it for the long term and make sure that you give your twelve hours or so, and then take time off. Or take time after that death. Because if you don't you will burn out, and you will burn out fast.

LW: That's what I do. I take time off. When they called me the very same day that this last patient of mine died and they said, "I think I've got something for you," I just burst into tears on the telephone. I said "Oh my God, not now. I just can't take it."

BCM: *Good for you. You've realized that you do get to the edge.*

LW: Yes, I said, "Do you think I'm bionic or something? Get out of my life, I'm mourning."

DK: You know a lot of times a nurse will call Progressive Nursing Services and say, "I can't do it anymore." And I'll call them and talk to them. And it's amazing when you talk to people who are burning out. You can ask them, "What things did you enjoy one year ago?" And they'll say, "Well, I love plays, I love movies, I love dinner, I love going to the beach." And then you'll ask them, "In the past two months have you done those things?" And they will say, "No." And the truth is, even if you know that everyone out there is dying and it's breaking your heart, you still need to take some time and have fun.

LW: I find I've been doing more of that, going for the joy, after taking care of these patients. Because I've got to live my life. It's what *they* want. That's what *they've* taught me. Get out there and do it! Live!

DK: And we're caregivers and we give and we don't realize that if we're not careful we can give it all away.

BCM: *And it's not that the giving ever stops but how can you give them an empty cup if you aren't filling up? I know mothers go through this, there's always a little voice, the guilty voice, the little voice saying, ''You know, you may have just helped someone die, but you didn't do this, or you didn't do that.'' So how do you answer those little voices when you do take the time out to play, when you do take time out to take care of yourself?*

LW: I never feel like that about the patients.

BCM: *You never feel guilty about enjoying yourself even when someone you care about is dying?*

LW: Right. Because they want you to enjoy yourself.

BCM: *I needed to hear this. I want people to know the range of emotions that caregivers go through when they're dealing with this all the time.*

DK: I've had two experiences recently of seeing so many people around me dying that after a while I felt horribly guilty about enjoying myself.

BCM: *That's what I was wondering.*

DK: Absolutely. But as Laurie said, you realize that those people you love want you to enjoy yourself. And also, I've sat with people when they are dying and it's amazing. It's like a microcosm of the universe, the time seems to stand still sometimes, and there is such a sense, when someone's dying, of how precious life is. And then you realize that you need to enjoy life to its fullest. Every day, every second, every minute.

BCM: *That's the whole thing.*

DK: And even with my father dying in there in the other room, just what you're saying is true. Tonight I'm thinking of going out to dinner with friends. Well, I could sit here with him instead and ask myself, "Have I done enough?" Or if I go out, and he dies tonight, will I think, "God, last night I shouldn't have gone out to dinner to have a good time"?

BCM: *The last night of Michael's life I went home to my son's house in a suburb of San Francisco to wash my hair. And I thought then, and sometimes even now I think...*

DK: What kind of mother is *that*!

BCM: *I know! I wanted to meditate on the balcony to let him go, because I felt like even though we had been in acceptance since Christmas, and this was now July, and we all kept praying that God would take him out of his pain and misery, I had the sense—and I'm wondering if you all have had this sometimes too—that many times a patient chooses to go only when he is alone because people are holding him or her back. They feel "I don't want my mother to have to see this. I don't want to make it any harder on the people who are here." It's almost—especially since Michael was so considerate—as if he thought, "I will wait to die when they are not here to hold on to me in any way." Or maybe it's just a private thing.*

DK: Well, I'll tell you, it's often like that exactly. We've seen hundreds of patients at Progressive Nursing Services, and the reality is, I have seen lovers and parents who have been obsessed with being there for *that moment*. I have seen people who have not left the house for two months. The groceries, etc., everyone else is handling it so that they can be there for *that moment*. And I've seen it happen so many times, they'll be in the bathroom and then the dying one chooses to die alone no matter what. Either it is a private thing they want to go through or somehow internally they make a decision that it would be easier if mother is not right there at the bedside, or anyone else.

BCM: *And for some of them it's not that beautiful when they die. It's more like, "Do not go gentle into that good night. Rage, rage, against the dying of the light."*

DK: We tell people that if it's meant to be, you will be there at the time of death. And it doesn't really matter if you spend twenty-four hours there, you just look for the quality in your time together. You look for what you *do* have together.

BCM: *It's those issues of control. For both the dying and their loved ones.*

DK:　Right.

BCM: *I saw this with Michael. He was determined to orchestrate his funeral, his celebration party afterward, I mean every single aspect of his life. He was not going to give up control. And that was his great lesson in life: to surrender, to let go of that control. And a lot of times that's what the families are going through. They think death has to look a certain way, and it doesn't fit their pictures that they should be angry at this family member or that they should want to run wildly out of the house and take a two-hour walk, or that it is a very messy process sometimes, just like birth is.*

DK:　Exactly, and I think we often protect people from the reality of death. I know that my father's death and my being here with him now *looks* textbook wonderful. And I want to tell you that my father and I have had lots of problems and lots of issues, and there has been lots of guilt there and lots of agony. And when he was coming down here to spend time with me, I spent time with my therapist and I said, "You know I've been planning to have this talk with him and say to him, 'I love this and I appreciate this and I also want you to know that I'm real upset about this and I think that this was a horrible thing,' etc., but how can I say this to him now because now death could be around the corner and besides he's eighty-three years old!" And my therapist and I talked about this, about how there's a difference between getting something out and getting even.

BCM: *Very good point.*

DK: And it was important for me to get it out. Get it all out. Whatever I wanted or needed or desired to say to him. And it doesn't matter whether he may be dying or whether he's eighty-three. Once again you can't protect people from their own lives. And the reality was, I felt so angry about things, and he felt so guilty about things during our whole relationship. So I sat down and I told him all the things that were upsetting to me, and he told me some things that I had done that were so upsetting to him. And as much as I thought that would be such a horrible confrontation, my anger was gone and his guilt was gone.

BCM: *You cleared a space.*

DK: We cleared it, you know. And if you have something to say to someone, it doesn't matter if they're ninety-eight or if they're dying, say it!

BCM: *It's always like that. And then you have such a sense of completeness, as you and I were talking about earlier. So that's some valuable advice from someone who's been there.*

DK: Right. Learn the difference between getting even and talking it out, and don't feel guilty about getting it all out.

BCM: *What else?*

LW: You know, I think that there are some other things I have learned from death. You see, I was divorced when my kids were really young, and I did have some hard times with my children; what I called my little screamers with them, but we always talked. But now, taking care of dying patients, I've realized that I don't have to always be screaming inside, or screaming outside at other people either. So now instead of just yelling

and freaking out because of something that my
kids have done, I have the real ability to sit down
and discuss things with them in a loving way.
And that's what I think that death and dying has
done for me.

BCM: *You see that there's another way to do things.*

LW: There is another way to do things. And everything can be done through love. You don't have to
be destructive, you don't have to be hateful, you
don't have to be anything, you just have to discuss things.

DK: You just have to sing. (Laughter).

BCM: *What do you do when you have very stubborn patients*
that you can't reach with love? I'm reminded of some-
one I know who got even by dying. (Laughter). I mean
there are so many ways people stick it to you. How do
you deal with dying when it doesn't look like a beauti-
ful ending or everyone healing the relationship within?
I still have trouble with this. Not every death is ideal.

DK: True! We were talking about this very thing this
morning. When you go into someone's house and
into someone's life, as much as you may think
that emotionally you may have the answers for
them, or you could help them communicate better, or you could facilitate a more beautiful death
than the one they're having, you have to realize
that they have had years to develop their relationships. The reality is that Nancy Nurse walking in
twenty-four hours before someone's dying is not
going to change this person's dynamics.

BCM: *The families have to change it.*

DK: Right. And, if a family lived in anger and lived in
upset, that's probably just how the death is going
to be. And *that's* acceptance of death. We can't
only learn to accept beautiful death, we have to

learn to accept *any* death, and people tend to die the same way they lived.

BCM: *I have seen some remarkable changes occur in families when a death comes on the scene, and I'm also aware of what it involves, but, it doesn't always work out the way that it's supposed to.*

DK: Right. Well you know, I remember one example from when I was working at a hospital on the geriatric cases. There was a skilled nursing facility attached to the hospital, and there was an old man there who was really angry and very, very mean and I kept wondering "Have they mistreated him here, what happened here that has caused him to be so mean?" And his family came in one day and told me, "He's been mean all his life. This is *him*." (Laughter). We tend to think that what's going on *now* is what's determining the patient's emotions, yet people have had a lifetime to become who they are.

BCM: *Yeah, we always think everybody's so nice. I mean, isn't it that way? You go around thinking everybody on the face of this earth is full of love when it simply isn't true.*

DK: And the reality of it all is that someone got even with this, and then they got even with that, and so they may then get even by dying. That's like suicide. Suicide can be...

LW: A real get even.

DK: It can be one of the most selfish things that you can do to other human beings, or, I've seen it done in ways that it can be most beautiful.

BCM: *Yes.*

DK: And it *can* be someone taking control of their life by ending that life in a beautiful way.

BCM: *The work I'm doing on ways of handling death and dying and the grieving process has opened my eyes to the fact that there are just as many ways, and just as many reasons, for taking control of your life through the dying process as through the living process. There's a lot of ways to do it.*

LW: I know. This last guy that I took care of had already made a pact with his loved one that if they both got sick they would just end their lives.

BCM: *We were talking before about how your feelings have changed since you were working in Nursing school, yet it's been my understanding, and stop me if I'm wrong, that when you're a nurse or a doctor you pledge to save life no matter what. Keep people alive, no matter what they want. What is the reality? And how do your ideas change so that you know what is right about people living in such devastating ways, i.e., hooked up to life-support systems or in dementia or in great pain?*

DK: The first thing I've learned is that there is no right and wrong. First thing. The second thing is to go for the quality, and not the quantity, of the person's life. Because we have so many tools now and so many machines that are incredible. We can prolong and sustain life, but at what cost? And I mean both the emotional and the financial cost.

LW: Ultimately, it's supporting the hospitals, it's supporting the doctors. They sometimes don't care about the patient, they sometimes don't have any real feelings about the patient, as you know. You have just gone through it. Many doctors don't really care about the family members.

DK: Some of them don't.

LW: Why do they want to keep a person living?

DK: It is amazing to see the difference though, in my father's case. Dr. Steve Knight is taking care of my father. He has over 500 AIDS patients. So my dad's case is like one in a million for Dr. Knight.

BCM: *How can he have 500? How?*

DK: Well, hopefully he can keep them well so that they're not all in the office at the same time. (Laughter).

DK: But I'll tell you, the first thing he did with my father was to sit down and say, "Joe, tell me about your life. What do you want? How do you see it? What do you think about death?" It wasn't like with most doctors who say, "Here's surgery, here's confinement, here's the plan." Instead Steve Knight said to my father, "Joey, what's your plan?" It was incredible.

BCM: *Do you see the future turning more toward recognizing the right of the person to die at home, toward home health care, and the softening of these impersonal, mechanistic attitudes? Like when the old family doctor used to be there for the* person, *and for the whole family?*

LW: I guess we're turning to the old ways when people died at home with their family around and they were loved.

DK: We've totally avoided that in our culture. We've set up "funeral homes" because we don't want to keep them at home when they die. Now when they die we move them to a "funeral home" so that we can pretend they're at home.

LW: Right. I mean in the old days they used to have the casket, they used to have the viewing at home.

DK: And then they tell us they're just sleeping, they're not really gone. How can we deny death? It's such a part of life! It's just incredible to me. I think it's one of the most profound moments and we can be missing it half the time. There are two aspects I've noticed about dying at home. I've had patients in the hospital tell me, "If I can just get home to the things I love, to my cat, to my dog, to my neighbor, to my pictures, that's where my strength is. That's who I am. And that will help me recover." They find their healing strength at home. And then there are other patients who say, "I'm dying and it's time. Let me go home to the things I love. Let me die there versus these four hospital walls."

BCM: *How do you educate the families? This is such a cultural thing in our society. And it's such a hard thing. How do you help families even realize it is all right, that they can take care of someone at home? And then, of course they've got to get through all of their own feelings of inadequacy and ineptitude. I learned all kinds of things that I never knew.*

LW: Did you have nurses?

BCM: *The last four nights we had hospice attendants and we had a hospice nurse come in every single day to check on Michael, but we learned how to do everything that you do to take care of someone because Michael was a baby there at the end. And he was in a coma most of the time anyway. We don't really need to get into that. Michael died at home with his extended family there. Our family experience was that we faced such trials within ourselves. We were afraid we would hurt him, or we would do it wrong, because we were not trained to take care of a dying person.*

LW: Well, I was trained, but I was still not prepared.

BCM: *None of us are trained to even take care of our babies, much less somebody who is dying.*

LW: No we aren't!

DK: And, did anyone train you in life? Life is terribly hard and so is death. And I think probably some of the comfort is realizing that there are no great answers and there is no training and that whatever it will take you have within you.

BCM: *What about the families, though, that feel unable to take care of their loved one? Their fear is just too great. How are we going to educate a populace that it is a viable, valuable alternative to have somebody die at home with good nursing care or even, if there's not a possibility of that, partial nursing care, or just the family taking care of them?*

LW: You know it's hard for a family. It's really hard because in the hospital the nurses are so professional and so efficient and they bustle in and they are so starched. They bustle in and they bustle out, and they're so professional looking and you look at this in awe as a lay person and say, "My God, how do they know how to do that?

BCM: *How do they know what to do?*

DK: I know how it is. It's very intimidating.

LW: So you are intimidated. And when you're around these nurses, these nurses do really want to help you, I think. Don't you? I know *I* always want to help the family. And when I have a dying patient in the hospital, I spend a lot of time with that patient and whoever is there with them. Whether it be a spouse, a mother, a father, a brother, a sister, or a friend. I spend a lot of time with them and their families teaching them things. I start teaching them immediately. If the Hickman catheter goes in, then I start teaching them immediately about Hickman care so that if somebody tells them, "Oh, we're going to send so and so home with a Hickman," the family isn't saying, "Oh my God, do we have to learn this?" Because I've just been in there showing them. I start telling them about things like that. I start teaching them about nutrition. I start teaching them the importance of exercise. I start teaching them things about keeping their mind sane. And I spend a lot of time with these patients and their families.

BCM: *Where were you when so many of us needed you?*

DK: And there's the whole emotional side to getting people ready. I think we all do the most we can do. Of course if you're lucky, you have a nurse who is there and can say to the family, "You know, I don't know right or wrong here and this person's going to die, but I'll be here. I'll see it through with you."

LW: And then there are the patients who end up going home by themselves, because their families are afraid to take them home with them. Sometimes the families see this atmosphere in the hospital and they're afraid. They're so afraid! They say, "We can never do this!"

BCM: *And their own emotions are saying, "Help me, also!" When you are going through it all, you can hardly get up in the morning. And, you want to be there, you want to be there for the person, be there totally and unconditionally week after week. But then to have to learn new skills sometimes feels overwhelming, exhausting, impossible.*

LW: The hospitals need to take a good look at that too and start teaching the families, the caregivers, whoever is going to be with that person until he dies. And the ones who are teaching the families need to understand what they are going through at this time. That's one of the things that the hospitals need to take a good look at any time there's a death and dying situation. I mean, my God, let's teach these patients everything that they need to know, and start out simply where they don't feel like it's a teaching environment because people learn more quickly that way, you know, if it's just casual.

DK: For this very reason we have a program at Progressive Nursing Services that's seven weeks long and it's home nursing for non-professionals. It's a program for families and friends. It's great if someone doesn't have the resources of having nurses all the time and they need to learn more about how to care for the dying person. Or if they just want to learn more about how to be with someone when they're dying. How afraid you're going to be when the situation isn't in control and you're not going to know what *is* a medical emergency from what isn't. And how to go through what you don't know to what you *do* know.

BCM: *True. Very, very true.*

DK: The main thing we teach in that class is confidence. Because, I tell them in the beginning, the skills will be easy, you know, once you learn when to panic and when not to panic, what's natural and what's part of the process, you'll feel so much more in control.

BCM: *The bottom line in all of this is that we are in a process now, that death can, in a sense, be such a great teaching tool for all of us to learn how to be more complete human beings, how to deal with our own emotions and move through them, and our own fears.*

DK: And we are moving to a new level of understanding.

LW: And we are still learning. We are always learning.

BCM: *What is the most important thing you are learning?*

DK: Learning how to live — through the dying, just learning how to live.

BCM: *And just learning how to love. Understanding. Experiencing the love in all of this.*

LW: Oh yeah. Just experiencing the love.

The Gift
of
Guidance

SOUL SEASONS

The seasons within you come and
  go,
And who you are you do not know.

Your dreams must memorize the
  course
To lead you to a higher source.

You are the flower, you are the
  force.
You reap the harvest, shed the
  snow.

You are the one. You are the
  whole.
You are the seasons of your soul.

— BETTYCLARE MOFFATT

6

Cassandra Christenson is a registered nurse, Director of Education at the Los Angeles Center For Living, and host of the weekly cable television show "A Nurse Looks At Dying." A loving, light-filled woman, Cassandra calls herself "a midwife to the dying." She has produced a unique tape, A Guidance Through Death, to assist families and patients through this intense period in their lives.

Cassandra lives and works in the Los Angeles area but her tape and her message go all over the country to help the dying everywhere. The tape is reprinted here, following an interview with Cassandra. (*A Guidance Through Death may be ordered from The Los Angeles Center For Living. See ordering information in the resource guide at the end of the book. -ed.*)

As Cassandra and I spoke together, I was struck by her candor, courage and compassion. Her work with dying patients is a gift of guidance and a gift of love.

BCM: *Tell me about your work. You call yourself "a midwife to the dying?"*

CC: Yes, I'm like a midwife helping a baby through birth. I give advice for the actual caregiver and I give advice for the person to help them through death. It's imminent death that I work with. But my advice is not in the form of specific rules or ways to behave. What I try to do is help people stay open to what they're experiencing.

BCM: *What you're telling me is so important because it gets rid of the "shoulds" and the "musts," that people* should *die like this and it* should *look like this, and that the caregivers and the family should* do it in this certain way. *You know, America is sometimes like a how-to book. Just read a how-to book and you'll find out how to do it the best way. But death is so mystical and mysterious. It's also taboo in America. So we are floundering and don't know how to help one another get through.*

CC: Death is very, very profound and mysterious. It's such a mystery anyway, and then in our current cultural framework it's much more of a mystery because we don't *want* to even experience it. There's a whole atmosphere, beautiful and strange, which emerges when we just give it permission to *be*. America is very ignorant about death. In other cultures it's not so. And what worries me is that America is leading the world. So the world is being led away from a very organic, natural process that is not even "taught" in different cultures. For instance, I told a guy from Afghanistan, he asked me what I did for a living, and I told him, and he said, "We don't have that trouble in Afghanistan. When somebody is ill we all take off from our jobs, from whatever we're doing and we're with that person until they get well or until they die."

BCM: *How wonderful.*

CC: You see these are people that don't have to be taught.

BCM: *There's a sense of community instead of the isolation we have here.*

CC: Here we just take off. We hide. I met a guy from Nigeria who said the same thing as the Afghanistan man. He said, "We not only stay with them until they die, but we stay with them until they're buried. And we are in incredible pain for a day and then we joyously celebrate for a day." And to my understanding, the original Jewish law or teaching was not to leave anyone alone who is dying. I was talking to this Rabbi and he said that the modern day Jew is forgetting that, and they're just having someone be there *after* the death. So it's a very primitive, very organized, tradition that we as human beings are to be with someone who is ill. The change came as the western culture began to have this far advanced medical profession, this medical system that is fabulous, but has replaced the human component.

BCM: *It distances it.*

CC: So that in general, the family is treated as though they are a pain in the neck. And that is a tragic, tragic turn of events.

BCM: *Yes, it is.*

CC: So my teaching to caregivers is: *re-empower, re-invite* the family to be there. Help them to be there. It's scary. When I went out to be with David, he was dying out at L.A. County General, recently, it was scary for me and I'm a nurse of twenty-five years, and know exactly what to do. Well this didn't count. None of that counted.

BCM: *David was a personal friend of yours?*

CC: No, he was a client. I was called at the L.A. Hospice by friends and when I went out there, I'd never seen him and he did die a few days later.

And he said he had AIDS. He probably did, but he never treated it or did anything about it. And when I went out there his father and sister had just come in from Chicago. So I'm walking in there and he was in restraints, he was battened down really tight, all swollen and his breathing was very labored.

BCM: *Sad.*

CC: Awful. And nothing that I said let him know that he was loved, which is my work.

BCM: *That is the work, to let the person know they're loved.*

CC: Right. Or none of it counts. I knew that nothing there was what he needed. The most important thing is to be there and to just trust what is needed. But I thought "What is needed? *What?*" And when I tried to touch him I could just feel it wasn't appropriate. And afterwards I found out it took eight men to put this guy in the restraint. It took eight security officers and male nurses to put this guy into restraint, and he wanted the breathing tube out, he wouldn't let them put it in. The nurse who was telling me all this said, "That guy was so mad." He was so enraged, do you really think that he wanted some nurse that he didn't know to come and 'help?' So I felt when I was there, nothing I said counted. And I needed to honor the feeling I had which was a real sense of inadequacy. The next day the hospice called and said, "All you needed to do was just say," (which was what I did say) " 'I'm the registered nurse and it looks like you're very ill and we're going to do everything to help you and I want to just be here.' And then, just be there. And not try to touch." So, in some situations I know that that's exactly what I need to say and do. I will come in and say, "It's so important for me to be here. And we love you."

We are really missing out, as a culture and a people, in our love and our relationships and everything, by not being there in a loving way through death. And I have developed very specific things to do. Things that really help people say goodbye and tie up any of the last loose ends that haven't been taken care of. So that the person who dies knows: "I'm forgiven." And cherished. And they know their life is forgiven. The Guidance Through Death tape gives these kinds of reassurances and helps people let go. It's not religious, but I try to spiritualize the process. I mean, people are spirited. In order to die they need to be *in spirit*, and there are ways of helping people get there.

BCM: *Oh, that's beautiful. In-spirited instead of dispirited.*

CC: That spirit, that energy, will help a person to die.

BCM: *So, if the dying are unable to find spirit on their own, if they're scared, how do the caregivers help?*

CC: Friends and family can come all around to help that person. To dispel the fear. To give supportive energy. And with that energy a person is able to die. To leave. And I think when people become ill, generally they embark on a whole process in this culture which has been known to be a dispiriting process, and that is going to the hospital. So that as they become dispirited then you have this person near death who hasn't the energy to die. And so there's several things that help. Some people don't have that problem. They're in the beat, they're in the rhythm of themselves and of the universe to begin with. They live their whole life that way so that they won't have that problem, but many people do. And simple things like playing music can really help.

BCM: *Yes, we played beautiful tapes to Michael during the last few weeks.*

CC: And you still have to wait it out like the birth of a baby.

BCM: *You can't push it. We used all of these tools to assist Michael in flowing. Meditation, silence, touching, loving, music; there was even a point where, it felt like in retrospect, we were urging him onward. And there was still a tremendous struggle between him holding on and letting go. It didn't fit what we thought dying should be like. Going to the angels. It was a profound struggle.*

CC: There are lessons for all of us in death. It's all applied to the person who's dying. Who's taking us all through that process. They're really taking us through a learning process if we let them. But generally, I just don't think that our culture is prepared for that kind of work or learning. We're tidier, we're more efficient. Now they have medications to try to hurry birth, that's our mentality. And I don't think death should be hurried. It definitely has its own way. And I don't think that we should extend life. It's terrible when we try to play God. Death has its own way, and that's what I teach. To be gentle with the process. To allow that. Do everything that you can. I mean, what you did was just to surrender. Surrender.

When I was with Ray, whose story I tell on the Guidance Through Death tape, he had been unconscious for several days, and in great physical pain. His wife said, "Can't we do something? I don't want him to die." All the signs indicated death was near. He was dying of cancer. So I just encouraged him to die, to let go, and that's when he looked at me and said, "Are you trying to get rid of me?" So his was a very important lesson for me. Here I was, a caregiver, thinking I knew what was best for him. And he never did come through resolution. He felt that he would get better. Always. And that was just the way he was all his life. I had to honor that, that he had *his* way to die. Another thing I learned from that experience was that, Jean, his wife, needed to be supported so that she could be there. Jean sat there and told him that she loved him until he died. She told him all the things she loved about him. And I helped her to overcome her resistance to being there. Because she had a major resistance. His death reminded her of her mother who had died when she was three.

BCM: *It brings up all the other deaths to be resolved.*

CC: She did this journal writing, writing to Ray. Telling him why she was with him.

BCM: *So this is one practical process that you would suggest for the family members, to write it out, write it out, write it out?*

CC: Yes. There is a journal process where you write using both hands, back and forth, so that one represents the linear and logical left brain and one represents the child and the feelings.

BCM: *The right brain.*

CC: So I did that to work with my feelings about Ray. He died then, without resolution, but who's to say what resolution really is? He really wanted to die surrounded with love and knowing he was wonderful.

BCM: *And that's what he got.*

CC: He just wanted to love.

BCM: *That's what he got. He got what he wanted. Do you also use journal writing processes or other processes to help caregivers in their training?*

CC: Oh, yeah. All of these processes are very helpful for caregivers and families. One time it really helped me was before Carlene died. She is also mentioned on the tape. She was a patient I felt very close to. The Friday before she died I was going off duty. I looked over and she looked like she was dead. I mean it looked like she was dead, totally. And I went over and I grabbed her and I said, "Carlene, wake up, wake up!" You know I just shook her like that.

BCM: *Why? Was it just instinctive?*

CC: Yes. It was a gut reaction. Instinctive. I felt that she should die with the family there, and none of them were there at that moment. I felt that it wasn't time for her to die. Who knows why I did it? You know, it was just a gut thing. I probably wouldn't react that way now. So I called a friend and she said, "Okay, you obviously don't want to let Carlene go. Let's do a process on that." And what I saw was that it was easy to let patients go in the hospital, where I only got to know them a little bit, but to let Carlene go when I had been with her and developed a close, intimate relationship over a two, three month period, that was very different. So I did a process where I talked between the left and right, the part that didn't want Carlene to die and the part that did. And the part that *did* said some extraordinarily difficult things to hear. My little selves were saying "I don't want her to die. I don't want her to live. I don't want to this, I don't want to that." There was even an issue for me about leaving a job when she dies, losing a job. My inner voices said, "I'm not getting it, I'm not being successful."

BCM: *A successful caregiver saves the patient, that type of thing?*

CC: Right. You can't let death come. But this was coming from the primitive part, from doing the left hand writing, and the other part was saying, "Why did you do that?" All the unmentionable thoughts that we as caregivers have inside came out.

BCM: *What you are saying for caregivers is very valuable. There are so many mixed messages and motives coming from the people who are there for the person. Several other caregivers have mentioned the fact that often people don't die while the family is there. It's almost like they wait until they have a private place, a space, to let go. Have you seen this happen before?*

CC: Well I think again, it goes back to the mystery. We don't know. We try to make sense of something and we can't. One thing that I've seen over and over, though, which makes sense to me, is that there are some common dynamics. For instance, dying people want to spare our feelings. But I see both. I see people die when a person is there, and I see people that die when no one is there. My friend's daughter was dying and she just went to the bathroom, and when she came back her daughter was dead, it just devastated her. But I just think that we have to be aware that sometimes the dying person may not want to let their loved ones down. They may feel it's too hard for the person to see them die. We're not talking about a *conscious* decision. It's an unconscious thing. Love does sustain life. So that when Ray was dying, one nurse had her hand on an artery, and when Jean kept saying, "I love you," Ray's heart sped up every time she said it. And then when she stopped, the heart slowed down and he started to die. And she'd say, "I love you." So love, prayers, presence can sustain life and sometimes they enable the person to die. And sometimes I think maybe the person needs to just be alone in total quiet, total peace. So as caregivers we need to support what that person needs who is dying. It may be that they want to be alone. And then we need to support the poor family who may be feeling like they somehow let the person down. Because often what gets left is people's guilt and devastation that it wasn't done right, that they should have done something different. And that's one important thing that a professional caregiver can do, and that's to help the family know that they did the best they could, and their love is what's important. I believe that the way a person is dying is the way they need to die, whether it's alone or with someone. The family needs to know that too. My friend Helen, who is a therapist, acts only as a support for the family. She doesn't even come near the person who's dying. She comes in and she helps cook, she helps clean, she helps do all the things so the family can be there with their loved one. But occasionally the most supportive thing the caregiver can do for the family is to take their place. Because the family and the loved ones can't be there. They can't do it. Or at least not twenty-four hours a day.

BCM: *We had hospice people for the last four nights. And that relieved us.*

CC: On the other hand, I think one of the most important things for professional caregivers is *not* to take the place of the family or of other loved ones *psychologically*. And sometimes family is no longer family, that's a whole other issue to be aware of. There are people now that are dying who do not have ties to their family anymore. But I think that we as professionals must surrender to the ones who are dying and allow them to choose who they want to be there. And, sometimes the caregiver needs to be a negotiator and a diplomat because people may be flying in from Chicago and they don't know what's happened in this person's life. And they have equally as important needs to be there. So, in my work as a helper, I come in and I work with everyone who wants to be there. What I do and what I teach other health care professionals to do in hospices is to get together with everybody who wants to be there. And we talk about what everybody wants for that person who is dying. We also talk about what everybody wants for themselves, which is equally important, because that person is going to die whereas these people are left with a lifetime of memories to cherish. So we talk about that and then I support them and empower them to do what it is they need to do, and not to give up control in the situation.

BCM: *Right. Because there are often a lot of control issues involved.*

CC: Well, the pain and the grief is not okay is how most of us feel in our culture. So we feel anger and pain. So there's a lot of rage or anger and irritability. And natural anger. It comes out. And as a professional you need to honor each person's way and allow them to be there in that way. As an example, one time I was working with about twelve people. There was a lot of rage. And when we left after two hours of being together, each person knew that they would need time there by themselves with the person who was dying. And that they would be able to be there and that their way counted. So the thirty-year-old son, who was a dynamo, was given permission to not be there and to just do what he did well, which was to organize. He did all the organization, and it was his way of doing something important.

BCM: *And it was okay.*

CC: It was okay. He didn't have to spend any more time in there, he didn't have to feel guilty. His way was very important. And the daughter that wanted to be there and really talk about her mother's death with her, was given that permission, to be there. And everybody could see the importance of her part there. Each person had their own way and was acknowledged to do that way. And given time to be there. So that, as a caregiver we empower the family and the cherished ones. We empower them and give them permission to be there in their own way and stand up for them. So that when that person dies, it's not me, the caregiver, that's there. It's the family or the ones that are really important to the person.

BCM: *The sensitivity that is required is just incredible. You can't go in there and do it or manage it or anything like that. You can't take it over for the family.*

CC: You can't even teach them how to do it. Like the analogy of the midwife of the dying to the midwife of the birth is that the midwife can't just come in and take over and give birth to the baby. The mother does that. And the baby that's being born. So my job is to be there in the most gentle way to *facilitate*. To *suggest*. What it really boils down to is. . .

BCM: *Not being directive?*

CC: Right.

BCM: *So you act as a gentle loving guide, and people can read that and then follow their own way. Don't you feel, though, that people do need guidelines since people don't talk about death in our culture because they're so afraid of it?*

CC: You absolutely have to have it. You have to have specific ideas on what to do. For instance, to repeat yourself, to speak simply, to express your love verbally or physically; it just helps the family if they have some notion of what to expect. Because something extraordinary happens in a dying person. And this person needs to integrate what's happening for them and what their relationship to it is. One important thing is that at the end there's a lot of whatever the dying person needs. Whatever they need. And if being there as a caregiver to role model for the family helps, then that's great.

BCM: *Caregiver as a role model? That's something I hadn't heard before, but it sounds really ideal.*

CC: One of the main things I teach is to touch. For patients, hold them in a rocking chair and rock. There's a nurse at St. John's or Santa Monica Hospital that did get into bed and hold the person as they were dying. There's the man in the Shanti Foundation who, when a very loved one was dying, he ordered another hospital bed and put the two together. So these are things I teach and on the other hand, some people don't want to be touched. I just use that as an example of, yes, there are guidelines, but there really are no "shoulds." One guy told me, "When I was with my loved one I was wondering, 'Now what would Cassandra do?'" And it shouldn't be that way. I don't want to be a role model in such a rigid sense as that.

BCM: *How do you manage day after day, week after week, month after month and get past the burnout or past the fear or past the this or past the that, past the ego into that place where you can really be of service?*

CC: I let myself feel intensely in any kind of situation. I take time after the death of a person. I take time for myself afterwards and I just wander. I'll go shopping. I'll go window shopping. I'll just wander through downtown or I'll just idle. One thing is, I can't go back. I can't, for instance, keep in touch with the family. I give totally when I'm there. I can't give anymore than I do now. I can't.

BCM: *It's like a closed chapter.*

CC: Um hmm. I know it sounds awful.

BCM: *No, it doesn't. It doesn't sound awful at all.*

CC: So that's how I cope. I give myself plenty of warm baths and I smoke. And it's absolutely imperative to take care of yourself. I do a television show, and this one woman called who was totally demolished by this one experience she had taking care of a woman who died. And she left the profession, the medical profession, because of that. She could not stop caring. The other woman died and she had such grief, such pain, that she couldn't stay. So we need care, as caregivers. And we need support groups. We have them now at the Center but very few people come. I think that they're so burned out, they're so busy, that the support needs to come where they can get it. They can't be driving to the place.

BCM: *I experienced burnout, in a sense, with the Mothers of AIDS Patients group that I helped co-found here in Los Angeles. I'm not real active in it now, because after a year and a half of counseling, supporting, I needed to change to something else that is helping in another way, but is not like a rerun of the same record.*

CC: See, that's a very good example, what you're doing, and all caregivers need to do what you're doing. See, you could feel guilty about not being as involved with MAP, but what you're finding is that you've served, and now you're moving on to service in a different arena that is going to bring concepts to a larger audience and help people who you wouldn't be able to reach if you had stayed where you were. That's what I've done in a way, too. I cannot stay in a hospital, I just don't work well in a hospital. I need to be able to have all the time I need, a quiet gentle environment to do my work. I need total time to be with that person. I can't do that in a hospital. So I could feel guilty that I don't work within the hospital, and with the system, or I can acknowledge it and say, "This is what I can do and this is what I will do."

BCM: *And you can be at peace with yourself because guilt is the most useless emotion in the world anyway. And when do any of us ever feel that we are "enough?" I mean, even when we give one hundred and ten percent, we never quite do "enough." There's always such a need out there.*

CC: And you never know if you're doing the right thing. One-third of the time I worry, I think, "Did I do it wrong?" If you're going to do this kind of thing, you can be sure that you're going to do wrong things. And you won't be sure whether you're doing the right thing. Yet, you have to be in charge. Because if you're not, who is? You're not going to be able to do what you think you need to do if you don't feel confident. You have to be powerful, you have to be a negotiator, you have to be a diplomat, to work with the nurses and the doctors, and on the other hand you have to be open, helpful, and extraordinary. And sometimes in difficult situations you even have to be conniving, to get what you need for this person. And I'm constantly afraid. I just say, "Show me the way. Show me the way." I'm so vulnerable. One family, the family I told you about, was saying, "Why do we have this nurse here? We are coming to see the doctor. What are you here for?" The patient and the situation was like a projection for their anger. I just kept listening until I heard all the facts. Then I knew the lay of the land. What needed to get said, and what needed to get done. That's why I let the patients and the families talk. So if I hear Ray say he's gonna get well, then I'm talking in that language. If it's a born-again Christian I talk a little more in their language. What they can understand. Not phony, but just communicating.

BCM: *You align yourself with that part of the person.*

CC: Yes. And I, as a helper, can sometimes perceive things that they can't. I try to discern what they think is going to happen. Do they foresee miracles? Do they have a Jewish orientation, or a born-again Christian one, or an agnostic one? I listen more than I talk, so that they're not hearing another expert.

BCM: *Somebody else talking at them.*

CC: That's right. That's right.

BCM: *But to get back to the issue of burnout, you talked about some of the ways that you nourish yourself. We must know what we can and cannot do and take care of ourselves. Do you have any other advice for caregivers as far as how to keep from going under?*

CC: Well, my main work is helping people through death. But, as a caregiver, I'm *also* helping this wife, this mother, this child; the relatives of the person who's dying. And I help by respecting their way of operating. What they are going to give is most helpful if they can just be themselves. That is, I think, the most important thing. So that they're not pushing themselves to do something they just can't do. And then feeling guilty because they couldn't do it.

BCM: *I know from my own personal experience, and my work with the Mothers of AIDS Patients group, that many mothers have a hard time with the guilt. You're the mother and you're there to take care of your child, who is like an infant by the time he's down to eighty pounds, and it's up to you to shelter him and protect him and keep him from dying. And to move from that place of healing, from being the caregiver that protects, and kisses it and makes it well, to the letting go of the child, I think to me is the most difficult thing. Because there is a complete switch. It's love both ways but it's a complete 180 degree turn.*

CC: And what the mother is going through is the same thing that the nurse goes through in a lesser degree. So it's a very important issue. And I think that what we're called upon to do is to play a number of roles. Because that person that's down to eighty pounds and dying, in addition to being a child, is also a man. The whole man is there. And I have to see that when I go in with all those dying men. Most nurses see little dying men and I want to see that strong male that's there. He just isn't available to my naked eye. But he is there. And I think as caregivers we need to recognize all components of the individual, and have some respect for how people were in their prime, so to speak. So as a mother *or* a caregiver, we need to recognize all that is within the person. It's hard. Very hard.

BCM: *What haven't we talked about that you would like to say?*

CC: Well, the most important thing is what I did with Carlene, which was to help her to know she was safe.

BCM: *Safe. I love that word.*

CC: And she was loved. She had abandoned her children when they were two and three years of age and she needed to know she was forgiven.

BCM: *Absolutely.*

CC: And who else was to say it? The priest had come in and left in minutes. As she was dying I said, "Carlene, you did a good job." I said, "Just getting through your life was a good job." She needed to hear those things. I also say to families, "Approach this time as though you're a scientist. A detective. And look and see what it is you see." Because, as I mention in the Guidance Through Death tape, Carlene was having a little dry run; certain out-of-body experiences. One guy told me, "I went to Egypt. It was real." And I think it's the psyche's way of preparing, I think the person dying does a lot of inner preparation. We can help the person overcome the fear and understand that the psyche or the internal self, or whatever that is, prepares us, helps us through this process. One man who was dying in the middle of the night said, "I want my bathing suit and my sunglasses." So they put that on him. And then he sat there and he looked at this blank wall and we said, "What are you looking at?" And he said, "The sunset, look at that. It's so beautiful." His mother, his sister, and his friend got in the bed and we all sat there and watched the sunset.

BCM: *Beautiful.*

CC: So again, it's talking in that person's language. My friend Elizabeth, when she first came back from being with her brother Dennis, who was dying, she told me all about it. He would say things to her like, "The brakes, I didn't set the brakes." So she left the room and went out and came back and said, "I took care of the car, don't worry about it." You know? "I took care of it." I mean she worked with his language. She didn't fight it. It's very important to believe what the person says and to listen, so that then this extraordinary experience of all the things that they're seeing can be shared with another person. And it isn't so scary, you know. It's an incredible thing to sit there and believe *with* them. To get a taste of what they're going through. Some nursing literature says, "If the person is talking irrationally try to get them to be in the here and now." Well I don't believe that.

BCM: *We didn't correct Michael, but I don't know if we went along with it.*

CC: I don't want to make you wrong in what you do; each situation is different.

BCM: *No, I'm just remembering when he would go in and out of dementia. You know we promised him he would die at home. And at one point, he was convinced that we had erected a stage set for him in that bed and put all the flowers and the candles, and Nancy's beautiful white Austrian linens and bedcoverings, that we had done all this to fool him into thinking that he was dying at home. He was afraid that he was really dying in the hospital.*

CC: So he was a perfect example of where you had to bring him back to reality.

BCM: *And we just kept saying, ''We're here for you Michael, and we love you.''*

CC: These stories are so important, because for every example I have of a way to do something, there's often an example that's exactly the opposite. Yours is a perfect example of how you had to do things to help Michael realize the reality of him being home.

BCM: *That we were there.*

CC: Oh, you had to. And that was what I did when I went to see David, the man I mentioned before. I said, "I'm Cassandra. It's ten in the morning. It's Saturday morning, it's a beautiful day. You're in the intensive care unit." There are certain things that you need to say to keep the reality. So it's an extraordinary dance that you're doing of, "Yes, this is true." "That's not true?" "No, *this* is true." You want to acknowledge their reality and also remind them of *your* reality. You want to keep the communication and the connection going.

BCM: *And one way we can do that is to just be there for the dying person in openness and love. Your tape, A Guidance Through Death, really helps people to do that, and it's something I would like everyone to experience.*

A Guidance Through Death

Reprinted by permission of
Cassandra Christenson, R.N.

For the Family

Hello. I'm Cassandra Christenson. I'm a registered nurse, and for many years I've been helping people when death is very near.

I'd like to help you. Help you to be there in a loving, supportive, guiding way, so that death comes in a gentle, reassuring way, without fear and without pain.

In my experience over the years I have seen that death is very gentle and that the only thing that keeps it from being that way, is that we just get so scared. We don't know what to say or what to do, and we abandon the very one we care so deeply about.

So let me encourage you, invite you, to be there, right up to the last moment of life. It's very simple, and of course it's very difficult. The difficultness comes because we want to run, we want to turn away; it's too painful. And the simplicity is that the only thing that's needed is your presence. To put that bed railing down, to draw your chair up close, to sit very near, and to talk with such intimacy, such love. The edge of life is a time of lovers. It's a time to cherish that life so deeply.

Now in order to do this you must really value you, and your own way of doing this. For some it's to bring humor, and looking back over life, talking about the things that you loved in that person; talking about even the little details that you so appreciated. For others, it is a quieter way. To simply be there, near, and letting the person know that you're there. Because when people are very ill sometimes you need to really say very clearly, in simple language the obvious, "I am here, it is daytime. I'll be here for two hours. If you need something I will get it for you. Trust me. I'm so happy to be here with you." And then, be very quiet. For others it's to come in very briefly, and have that close conversation, those close words. They may say, "I'm so glad I could come in. It's only going to be for a few moments, but you're in my heart. I think about you all the time and I'm sending you love. I just wanted you to know that I was near you, even though I can't stay for but a moment." And for others it may be to sit in the corner, reading, dozing at night, crocheting. Each person has their own way. It may be to take care of all the business that needs to get taken care of, and you may never go into the hospital. But if you can you will have one of the most profound experiences of your life, as you help that one you love, that cherished friend, that cherished family member, through the end of their life. The most important thing to do is to reassure. And when you do, you may think, "How can I reassure someone when they're dying? How can I say they're safe when it's the end of life?" I don't know how you can say that, except that in all the time I've been working with people, I've found that when we're able to overcome our fear, and wanting to run away, that there is so much life there. So much vibrating, pulsating life. And the most magnificent experience that I've ever had—over, and over, and over. Let me give you an example. Last night Hilda was dying. I went to her home. There were many family members there; maybe ten. Some were in the front room sleeping and others were watching television with the sound turned way down. I came into the room about 9:15, went straight to Hilda, who was in quite a contortion. She had far advanced cancer and she was unconscious and her body was drawn up in continuous spasms. I went straight to her, put my arms around her and started to cry and said, "Oh, Hilda, I'm so happy to be here with you. I love you so much." And I just looked into her face with so much love. I love her so much. And then I talked casually with her family, saying the things that I knew were important that we talk about, and that Hilda could hear even though she was unconscious. And I held her hand and I stroked her hair. We wanted Hilda to know that I knew death was near. I wanted her to know that her family was planning for her to go to the hospital the next morning, so that if she wanted to die at home, she was going to need to do that soon. I wanted her to know that her mother and her aunt were coming from the East Coast on Saturday so that at some deep level, if she needed to wait for them to come, she would know when they would be there. And every once in a while the tension would get stronger, and at those times I'd say, "You're safe. You're loved. You're safe, it's O.K., it's all right. I know Hilda, it seems like you're dying but I think you're getting born. You're very safe." Little by little, her muscles began to relax and at one point she drew up suddenly and I heard the body making noise, like the intestines were gurgling and I began to hear some gurgling in her lungs, and I knew that her death was very very close. And I just kept saying, "You're so loved, it's O.K., it's O.K., it's all right." And then she opened up her eyes, and she looked over at her sister Mary, and her muscles began to really relax. And I motioned for everyone to come near and to put their hands on her, to touch. And Mary called in the rest of the family. And everybody was around the bed, touching some part of her, and I knelt down at the foot of the bed, holding her foot. And she smiled, and looked at each person in the face, and then died.

The touching is important with most people, though some people would prefer not to be touched, and then it's important to just be near. And yet, even people who have not wanted to be touched in their life, generally when they're frightened need to be held. Some people

believe that if you touch the lower part of the body, it's
like death comes by going to sleep, and you waken
them by touching the lower part of the body, so it's important to keep your touches up on the cheek, the hair,
the hands, the heart. It's important to reassure. I know
that it's strange to reassure when someone's dying, but
every bit of my experience shows that death is very,
very gentle. There's almost a sweetness there. And people that have had near death experiences always say
when they've been resuscitated—people that have appeared to have died and then the physicians were able
to bring them back—always say that they would never
be afraid again to die; that it's like they were in the arms
of love, or there was this incredible light that they felt
so loved by.

Elizabeth went to see her brother on the East Coast.
He was dying of cancer. He was about 37 and had gone
from about 190 pounds to about 76 pounds, and he was
very afraid. They had never had a good relationship as
brother and sister. And when she went into the hospital
room he just kept saying, "Elizabeth, help me, help me,
I'm so scared, help me." And she just kept saying to
him over and over in very simple, reassuring words, "I
love you. I love you. And you're safe. Very safe." When
people are very ill, it's important that the language be
simple, and with some repetition. So over and over she
said, "You're safe." After about an hour and a half, a little smile came on his face, a sigh, and he said, "I'm
safe." And Elizaabeth said, "You know I don't even
know why I said this Cassandra, but I said, 'Do you see
the light? Tom, do you see the light?'" And she told me
that with his eyes wide open, he looked up at about a
forty-five degree angle and he said, "Yes, I think so."
She said, "Well, do you think we can get to it? Can you
get to it?" and he said, "I think so." And then she said,
"Well hold my hand; we're going to walk into that

light." And then he reached up and grabbed her and pulled her down over the side rail, because she hadn't put that down, and held her with such intensity and said, "I love you," and then said, "Oh my gosh—I see the light. I see the light!" and started clapping! And Elizabeth said, "*What* is going on?" And he said, "But they're all here. They're all here!" And he mentioned Uncle Charlie and Aunt Susie and people that she didn't even know, but she later found out that they had died before. He clapped for ten minutes, and she clapped with him. And he said, "They're so proud of me. They're so proud of me." And after ten minutes, he stopped clapping and he got very very quiet. And she said, "What's going on now, Tom?" And with the most beatific look, this great big, formal, clumsy, upstate New York cowboy said, in response to her question of what's going on, he said, "Celebration. Celebration." And he died. This is what you can give to the one you love. You can help them through this passage, this event, this closure of their life, in your own special unique way. Whatever period of time, whatever way you need to be there. Another very important thing that Elizabeth did, and is important for us all to do is that when we're there, to not have any idea of what we're going to do. What we should do, what we shouldn't do. But to be there almost nakedly. To be there without any idea in the world what we're going to do. And for most of us that's very, very difficult. But it's important. Because it's only by not knowing what in the world you're going to say that you're able to be perceptive to what's needed to be said. And you're not always going to say the right thing. I'm right about one-third of the time, and about one-third of the time when I'm with someone at death, I'm not sure whether I've done the right thing. And probably one-third of the time I goof. I make a mistake and don't say the right thing. The most important thing is to be there. And to be there without any guidelines. Then you can say and do what's necessary. What will help that person. Elisabeth Kubler-Ross says just sit there. Don't feel like there's anything you have to do.

An example of when I did something that wasn't the right thing. Ray was unconscious for about five days. He hadn't said anything, he hadn't responded. He was dying of cancer. And his wife Jean said, "Cassandra isn't there anything you can do to help Ray? Help him to let go." And she said, "look at him. He can hardly breathe, he can't eat. Just help him to let go." So I said, "Ray, it's O.K. You can just let go, it's all right." And he opened up his eyes and he looked straight into mine and he said, "Cassandra, are you trying to get rid of me?" So that's an example of how if we're going to go, to be with someone who's close to the end of life, and we're going in without any definite guidelines, we're definitely going to make some mistakes. And it's O.K. Because the most important thing is for you to be there in this way. And out of that mistake I thought about how of course Ray wouldn't want the nurse to tell him to let go, Ray would want Jean to be there with him. His wife. And Ray wasn't the type to let go. He was a fighter to the last breath. So what Jean did is for the following five days she sat near to him and told him everything she loved about him. All the wonderful things that she loved. Very specific things. How she honored him and held him in reverence. I remember one night I came in about three o'clock in the morning and I said, "Jean, this room is so filled with light." She said, "That's love Cassandra, it's filled with love."

Carlene is a woman I cared for about 1978. I was doing regular nursing. And she said to me, "Cassandra, when I get real close to the end of my life will you be there? And will you talk me through it?" So when the end was very near her husband and her daughter and her granddaughter and I sat on the bed and we did just that. We talked her through it. It took forty-five minutes. In forty-five minutes she was gone. And I thought to myself, this is what people need. I remember seeing a documentary about Florence Nightingale. I remember that as hard as she worked in the day time, she'd come back at nighttime with her lamp because she said, "No man is going to die alone." And we don't do that with our own loved ones. We have the advances of modern medicine, and death is often in isolation. You and I can make a difference, and you, right now, can make a difference. Don't give up on that one you love. Don't give up on yourself either. Because you've got to pay attention to what you're able to give, in the way you're able to do it. Nurture yourself, take care of yourself, value yourself. Appreciate you, and what you need. And then you will be able to be there fully. Fully, completely, when you're there. I also want to encourage you to use whatever resources or help is available to you. If you're in the hospital, social workers can be of help to you. The Chaplain, Rabbi. You might even go out in the hall and ask the nurse to give you a hug. It may help her as much as it helps you. Take time for you.

*   *   *

The next section is for the one you love when the end is very very near. You may want to get some ideas from it, so that you can be the one that says these things. Helping someone through the end of life may be one of the most profound and moving experiences that you will ever have. And it certainly will be for the one you love. I encourage you, and support you, and if I may, give you permission to be there with gentle and tender intimacy. For you to be a guide, through this strange and foreign time. You can do it. I believe in you, and the power of your loving heart.

For the Patient

This is your time. A time of life. You are right now the most important person, and it is time that you take care of your own needs. You may feel that you are dying, but I have a feeling that you are getting born. My name is Cassandra Christenson. I'm a registered nurse, and I have helped people through their dying for many years. And in my experience, I've not seen death, only life. Can you believe me? As you get closer to the very edge of your life, it'll be very much like going to sleep. You will find that you drift off and then come back, drift off. During this time, be very aware of what's happening. You may see very vivid visions, dreams, or have odd happenings. For example, it may feel like you're really getting up and going to the kitchen to fix yourself a sandwich, or even walking outside, and dancing. I remember Carlene. Carlene asked me to be with her, and talk her through her death. And when the end was very near, she said, "Cassandra, I would've sworn I went outside and danced, and I've never danced in my life. It was so real." It seems to me, it seems as though we practice going in and out of our body, you know like stepping out of our body, and coming back in. It's like a practice, so that when we actually do leave our body, we've had some dry runs, we've had the opportunity to try that out. Does that sound strange, leaving your body? In all my experience in helping people to die, helping them through this passage, it looks like that's what happens. It seems as though our bodies are little coats, earth suits, that we wear about, while we're here in this life, and that when death comes, we step out, into the arms of those we love. That's why I want you to look. Look about you, and see who might be there to receive you, to help you. To be your midwife. To just help you on your next step. Have faith. Believe that you are very, very loved. And safe. How can I say you're safe when it feels like you're dying? You are safe. This may be the safest thing that you've ever done, and I say that from many years as a registered nurse helping people through this passage. You're very, very dear and so beautiful. Getting through your life is not easy. And you did it. We're all so proud of you, of the way you lived your life. People that you touched that you may never know. Have faith in *you*. Appreciate *you* for having just gotten through it. And know, that you sowed seeds, things that you said, little things you did. Things that you learned, and shared with another. That is your legacy. Oh, sure, there's lots of things that you've ached over. "Why couldn't, why couldn't I have done it differently?" Oh, forgive yourself! This is your time. Forgive yourself. You did the very best you could. And now let it all go. You're safe. Let it all go. You're safe. And loved. And so dear. Trust me. It's O.K. Believe me. It's safe, it's safe, it's safe—to let go. Let that death-like grip you have on life, let it go. Fall into the arms, fall into the arms of those that love you. Fall into the arms of love. Fall into the arms of God. It's safe. And you're so loved. It's all right. You can let go, and know that you've done the best you possibly could. Is there anyone you need to forgive before you go? Think back. Is there anyone to whom you need to say, "I hurt so much because of what you did. And I forgive you."? Pain and suffering are difficult. Death is a graceful step through an open doorway. You are safe, and so loved. Don't be frightened when some very real dream comes, or vision, that seems so real, and so cockeyed—that doesn't seem like it could possibly be—don't be frightened. You're in the arms of love. Feel that, and know that. Trust me. Please. Believe. You're safe. And be like an explorer. Like a child of innocence, and wonder. And just watch what's happening around you. Don't get scared. This can be an incredible journey. Allow me to help you through it. You can let go. It's all right. Let go. It's safe. You're safe. And you're so loved. Treasure this time. It's your time. Believe me. This time is very gentle, like the wings of a bird. Enclosing you with love. You will step through an open doorway into such light! Do you see the light? Can you look around? Can you see it? Look for it. Do you see it? I want to hold your hand, and let's walk into the light. It's O.K. (laughing). Ohhh, stretch in the light. This is your time. You're so loved. So cherished. And you are forgiven. You're forgiven. Have courage. Let go. You're getting born. It may feel like you're dying, but you're getting born. Mmmm, you're getting born. You don't need that old raggedy-taggedy earth suit that you've worn around. It doesn't work anymore. It hurts. It doesn't work well at all. You're so much more than it. And now it's like—may I say—almost like graduation. Let go. It's O.K. It's all right. You're so loved. So treasured. You're so beautiful. I love you. We all love you. Don't give up on you. Don't give up on you. Know how very, very important you are. We're here with you. To help you through to your next life. And this one will be full of wonder. And of love. It's O.K. You can let go, and know it's safe. You're very safe. Trust me. You are so loved. Be like an explorer. Look around in your mind's eye, with your eyes open, and see who's there to help you. You're not alone. You can feel good about your life and what you've given. Sometimes those little things you never even gave a second thought about, are some of the most important gifts you could have possibly given. Ohh, my, you can be proud of yourself. Having gotten through this life was hard. Wrapped in the arms of love. Really. Can you feel that? Just drifting, very much like a young child drifting off to sleep. Aware of your loved ones that are around you, touching you, holding you, whispering into your ear. Sitting over there in the corner, sending their love to you. People that were not able to come but hold you in their hearts. People concerned about you, sending their love. It's all right. You can let go. You've done the best, the very best you could, with the circumstances and the situations that you had, the talents, you did the best you could. And now, you can let go. It's O.K. Maybe just before you go, you'd like to open your eyes and look around and see who's with you. Smile. And then close your eyes and let it all go. This is your time. A time of gentle endings. A time for new beginnings.

The Gift
of
Caring

POEM FOR JAMAL

The caregiver
       and the client
       who is the giver
       who is the taker
       which of the two is dying
       which of the two is truly alive
       which of the two
              sleeps soundly
       which one can
               dream with the saints
       which of the two serves
       which is healed
       which is sick
       which is healthy
How often
       I asked my-Self
               these questions
       how noble I once thought
               my-Self to be
       until I realized my teacher lay
       there beside me
       sleeping peacefully
       sleep unstirred
       breathing rhythmically
       the universe at his command
       the Angels at his feet

I could never
          in a million years
          compensate him
          for I realized
          that he was truly alive
          in his dying
          (and I had been
                    dead
                         in my living)
It was through
          his illness
          that I began to
                         finally heal
          and through
          my friend
          Jamal's death
          that I
          was finally Born

                    — MICAEL TAPIA

7

When I see Stuart Altschuler, I want to hold out my arms and give him a big hug. A quiet-spoken, loving man, he exudes comfort. Somehow I feel, after talking with Stuart, that everything is going to be all right, no matter what is happening in my life, or the lives of those around me.

Stuart is Executive Director of The Los Angeles Center For Living, and I interviewed him at the Center on a day when the place was full of activity. There were classes, private sessions, people eating lunch, and a piano playing in the next room. The Center seemed, as always, to be full of light, energy, and a joyful intensity.

The first question I asked Stuart before we began our conversation was: Just what *is* the Los Angeles Center For Living? Here is a description of their work:

The Los Angeles Center For Living is a community sponsored, non-profit organization dedicated to a spiritual and psychological change in our relationship to sickness and death.

The experience of sickness need not be hopeless. The experience of death need not be devoid of the dimension of joy. One day, and it is fast approaching, we will have transformed these experiences through the power of love. Health care workers, psychotherapists, clergy, families, body workers, artists, educators, spiritual counselors, musicians, and others—any and all people who feel moved to contribute their own resources of time and kindness—form this community of comfort and support for those who grieve. As we help others process sickness and death, we find ourselves experiencing our own emotional healing. For it is in healing others that we are healed.

The diagnosis of a life-threatening disease can be a tremendous emotional blow—to the patient and to his or her loved ones. The Center exists to support people through this experience. Its staff represents a team of men and women whose everyday professional experience provides them with substantial background in the areas of illness and grief.

Hospice philosophy has guided our goals. The underlying notion which inspires us is that peace of mind can be achieved regardless of physical conditions. Although we are not a bedded facility, we feel that, as an activity center, we can still contribute greatly to the peace and comfort of those who are dealing with the reality of illness or grief. From early every morning to late every evening, we are committed to providing a beautiful and loving environment for those who need us.

The Los Angeles Center For Living is a place of joy. It is a place where people can laugh, share, cry, listen to music or just sit by the pool and relax. If you or anyone you know is facing any aspect of serious illness or grief, please know that the Center is here to serve you. Come by and partake of our activities. Or just come by, spend the day and soak in an atmosphere of warmth and acceptance. *(See Resource Guide at the end of this book for address and phone number. -ed.)*

In this dialogue, Stuart speaks about feeding the spiritual, emotional, psychological, and physical needs of dying clients, as well as caregivers.

BCM: *I have been talking to everyone I know about something that has happened to me, which is that after you experience someone dying, you can actually feel their energy becoming a part of your life or a part of your service to life. It feels to me as though all the superficial stuff just dissolves away. That's a part of the celebration, and that's a part of the clearing of a path. I'm wondering if this is common to other caregivers who work in death and dying fields.*

SA: These are professional caregivers we are talking about?

BCM: *Professional caregivers and family caregivers too.*

SA: Well, for those who are open to observing and experiencing what's really going on, I hear it over and over again, from the nurses I've worked with at hospitals, and from nurses and social workers that come here to the Center for our caregiver support groups. I hear stories similar to yours and I think it's one of the things that keeps people from burning out. They feel the high intensity of the energy surrounding this kind of transition. That is, they are not just looking at the dying process in terms of whether or not it's negative. Instead, they're actually there for service and to help create a joyful atmosphere. A peaceful atmosphere. The intense feeling of working with death can be perceived as fear or burnout initially, and then worked through to get to the other side of it, which is the clear intensity you and I are both experiencing.

BCM: *What does it take to get through the places of the negativity and the fear and the burnout surrounding the daily work of being with people who are dying?*

SA: What it takes is simply people who are willing to get through their own fears. Unless they do that, they *do* burn out real fast. Any unit in a hospital that is dealing with life and death, whether it's cancer or AIDS, or whatever, has a very special type of person working there. Or they don't last. They just don't last. The nurses, doctors, patients, it's just a different type of person there because it feels like this is their service. There are some people in some hospitals that just don't belong there and yet they're working in those units, and they don't last. And there are some hospitals where the energy just isn't that good. You can feel it when you walk in the door.

BCM: *Do you have some ideas on how we can continue to clear the way and to be of service?*

SA: Well, I think the more the community is educated, whether it's on issues of death and dying, alternative methods of healing, or opening to other possibilities about what death really is or isn't; the more they're educated the better it will be. And it doesn't matter to me what your belief system is about life and death, so long as you're open to knowing that it's a natural flow in the universe.

BCM: *You almost answered my next question when you talked about the natural flow of the universe. I was going to ask you what your own feelings about death are.*

SA: What death is to me, I get back to the word *transition*. It's both an ending and a beginning. For me it's the ending of one phase of our existence and the beginning of another phase of our existence and at the same point it's a *continuation* of that same existence. I don't know if I'm being clear. I find myself not so fearful of death anymore. Yet I still get very angry at the methods with which some of us go through that transition.

BCM: *Do you think that there are certain ways to die?*

SA: There's a part of me that tells me, whatever we're involved with at this point is perfect for what we're supposed to be doing within ourselves and another part of me that still gets really angry when I see the kind of pain and suffering that we've got to do. Sometimes I get scared that I might create that suffering in my life at some point. I mean, I'm still going to my classes. I'm not totally clear, or totally balanced spiritually or emotionally about all this. This is one of the beauties of the Center for me because I come in here every day, and even when I worked at West Covina Hospital, most of my healing concerned those that were courageous in their way of reaching death. They were inspirations to me. And there are people who are inspirations to me right now. And so I came in here today as I do everyday and I'm learning from everyone and everything around me as I focus myself in a place like this.

BCM: *It's an on-going process. It isn't that you can give a recipe to do this, take this three times a day and you will be healed of death or your fear of death.*

SA: I know what's working for me and I know that I'm in a much better place today with it than I was a year ago, but that doesn't mean I don't go through pain and I don't go through grief. I still do. Daily. And it doesn't mean that I'm not going to hurt at times for myself as well as for others.

BCM: *I don't know about you, but the closer that I've been to death, the more human I feel, the more aware of the level of intensity of feelings that are a part of me in this lifetime.*

SA: Well, once again it gets back to the Center be-
        cause even though we're dealing with death, I
        have never felt so alive in my life.

BCM: *That's wonderful to hear.*

SA: Even though people are dying all around me, I
        am more alive today than I've ever been. I see the
        healing people do even when they make their
        transition, and I see the healing happening with-
        in the people that are coming here to the Center.
        I see some people who walk in here totally de-
        pressed, totally wiped out. People who were to-
        tally ready to give up a month ago are more alive
        right now than they've ever been. Because of the
        atmosphere that's here. Because of the love
        they're receiving. Because of the permission that
        they have here to feel what they're feeling and to
        get through it. (And the help they receive here in
        order to feel what they're feeling and to get
        through it.) We are not here for people to sit and
        wallow in self-pity. We're here for people to come
        and be who they are, to go through what they
        need to go through in order to feel okay about
        what is happening in their lives.

BCM: *It sounds like unconditional love to me.*

SA: Oh, very much so. That's true, even the volun-
        teers feel this. Even the volunteers who come in
        scared and wondering how they can help, they
        receive that sense of unconditional love for them-
        selves and others. They receive this when they go
        forward to embrace the issue of death instead of
        avoiding it. I have seen remarkable changes in the
        volunteers themselves. Because this is a place for
        living in unconditional love.

        We offer support groups especially for care-
        givers here at the center. I remember one social

worker who worked with hemophiliacs who have AIDS. She was thrilled to see that we were offering classes for people with life-threatening illnesses, but then she saw that we have a professional caregivers support group, and she said, "This is incredible, this is wonderful, now I have a place to go to get help and support." So she called this morning to confirm a space in one of the groups. We have three support groups for professional caregivers, to accommodate shifts. And those groups are just now beginning to take off. For a while nobody was showing up. They were too busy to take care of themselves. Cassandra Christenson has some different groups, aside from ours, which are run by licensed counselors. They're support groups for people who are dealing with the stress and the emotional difficulty of being around people who may be dying, who are ill. And they need a place to come to. People really need to realize and accept the fact that they can't do it all. We have another group which is called a caregiver's support group for non-professional caregivers. For husbands, wives, families, parents, whatever. It's for people who are there with the patient all the way through, who are hurting and need some care themselves.

BCM: *I know that you provide a place where people can talk about what they are going through and get clear on their emotions and go on to the next step. You provide for them a beautiful, healing, clearing place. But do you have any specific things that caregivers can do to keep from getting burned out?*

SA: Yeah, well I do have a few. Number one, don't isolate yourself. There are some people that do this and either do it because they like the martyrdom part of it, or because they don't realize that they have a choice. That they can ask for help, for support. We try and get them out of their loneliness, and help them see that there are other ways of handling the situation other than thinking that this is something God's laid on them. We all need to realize that people who are caregivers are human too. That they get tired sometimes and that is normal. They get angry at the situation and angry with the person they love dearly. They get angry at the fact that the person they love is dying, There is a rage inside of them about how it's affected their own lives.

BCM: *Yes, anger is such a no-no in our society. We're supposed to be so nice and controlled and loving.*

SA: People wonder how they can be angry at this person that's suffering. Well, it's just normal and healthy. And rather than holding it in and ending up subconsciously taking it out on that person that you're loving, or removing yourself and being destructive in other areas of your life, it's really helpful to be honest about it. It's safe to go to a place where there is a support group where you're going to find that other people in the same position are dealing with the same things. So, you know, I would definitely say to them, "Be more loving and accepting of what you're feeling and don't be afraid of it, and allow yourself to find an environment that will give you a chance to unload this, so you can get back and just be where you want to be, with that person you care about." That kind of balance is really important. And the other thing is, make sure that you are pampering yourself once in a while. Whether it's a nice hot bath or whether it's getting out or whether it's cleaning your room or whatever it is you love to do. Make sure in the process of healing that you can leave your site for awhile, that you can walk away from all the intensity for awhile. There are plenty of people who will be glad to come in and sit with the patient for a few hours so you can get out. There are some nursing services. And there are even volunteers. We have a few volunteers here at the Center that are willing to provide that service, kind of like a buddy program or helping sitters. Someone who is just a caring person who is going to sit there and be a companion to the ill person for a little while while the caregiver gets a break. It's the same thing with the parents. That's why we have special groups here that will allow children who have life threatening illnesses to be here, give their parents three or four hours away from the constant care.

BCM: *I'm glad you brought that up because I know that one of the focuses of the Center is to provide a space for everyone who needs nurturing. It doesn't matter how old you are or what disease you are confronted with. Are you using some of the principles we hear about in The Centers for Attitudinal Healing?*

SA: Well, those principles are integral to the general atmosphere of the Center, but we do also have a specific group. It's led by someone who was trained at Gerald Jampolsky's Center in Tiburon. Every other week we have the attitudinal healing support group here. So we are open to people with different approaches. What works for one may not work for another but we may have something else that will work for them. And, as you know, the Center was founded on the principles of *A Course in Miracles*, as taught by Marianne Williamson. We see that everybody has a different way of getting to the same ends. And a Center like this needs to make available those options.

BCM: *So in one sense you have a smorgasbord of healing opportunities here. We talked at the very first about all the physical bodywork that is available here in the Center. Now, what happens when someone comes in who is very ill and who hasn't been touched a lot? What happens then?*

SA: The bodywork appointments are constantly booked. It's rare that there is an opening, for that very reason. Very often when someone gets ill, either they're afraid of getting close to people or people are afraid of getting close to them. People don't know how to touch them, they don't know how to just be with them or hold them anymore. They're afraid of getting too close and "catching" the illness, even if they know, rationally, that it is not contagious. At war time, they found in orphanages where there were not enough caring people around, that the orphan babies weren't held and nurtured and so they died. They died that much sooner. And the same thing is true about adults who have life threatening illnesses.

BCM: *Yes. Skin hunger.*

SA: It's a skin hunger. And if they don't get that touching, then they're going to leave their body. If they're not reminded that their body is here, that people want to touch it and it's okay and that it's part of their loving energy, then they're not going to want to stay in that body. So we make massage available, as well as readings and classes and groups. A variety of resources. And it has made a total difference to some of the clients that come in here.

BCM: *What about caregivers? Do you have bodywork for caregivers who need to be touched and held and told that everything is going to be okay?*

SA: The bodywork is also available for the immediate caregivers. It's not there for someone who says, "Gee, my friend is sick and I could use a massage." There are too many people wanting bodywork sessions to really accommodate everybody like that. But if it's a husband or a wife or a parent that's just there constantly, and they really need it, then the bodywork here is available to them too. And we also are starting a lot more workshops that are dealing with touch and holding. These classes are listed on our monthly calendar. For example, Cassandra and I are going to be doing an every other week workshop that will be dealing with how to touch and be touched. It's a hugging workshop, to encourage giving permission to yourself to allow that touching, that warmth, and acknowledging your own need for it.

BCM: *And letting yourself be loved. That you're lovable enough that you too, as a caregiver, can benefit and deserve to be touched.*

SA: And then we have certified holistic bodyworkers who are going to do a four-hour workshop on the healing power of touch. The need for it in terms of nurturing. So we're incorporating more classes around that need here. We want to help people separate *sexual* touching from *physical* touching. A lot of people, especially when they get ill, find that they have a lot of issues around sex and sexuality and physicality; Where does it still fit in and where doesn't it? They're not sure. I'm just asking for a hug and then they think I want more so they're afraid of me. That sort of thing. So there are a lot of issues needing clarity which we hope to address with the workshops we're providing here at the Center.

BCM: *Well it sounds like every room is filled to capacity. I hear the piano going right now, and people singing. That's wonderful! I'd like to ask you now about the future. I know you're dealing with the immediate right now as you're helping in each moment right where you are. But does the Center also have a vision of the future?*

SA: I have a sense of where it's leading, but I've learned enough in the last two years to realize that it's not always our aimed-at, agreed-upon vision that happens. I'm learning to surrender to whatever is next. I know that we're getting busier and I know that at some point the facility we're in is going to be too small. And yet, even as I am already getting in touch with that, you know what I'm creating inside is a larger place that will still feel intimate and still have the same atmosphere. And so, hopefully we're not going to wait until it's on top of us and then start creating a larger space. Hopefully there'll be enough advance warning for us to incorporate our original vision into a larger vision. And I've really learned to just trust and know that as it grows it'll grow in the right direction. Because everything's been growing in our direction since we started. We've gotten such a positive reaction from the community, from APLA, Shanti, Aid for AIDS, doctors, the American Cancer Society, and certain cancer units at hospitals. They're just all really thrilled.

BCM: *So are you seeing a real change in institutional and public perception of life-threatening illnesses and how we should be dealing with it? Are we moving toward a model?*

SA:　I think so. I think that even the medical model is changing. I think physicians are seeing that what they do is not always enough and that they need some support to complement their skills too. And I've known a lot more physicians who are more comfortable and less ego-bound to say, "This is what *I* can do for you and I suggest you go to the Center here because they can help you with the other areas." And in a lot of ways, it makes the doctors feel that they are doing more than just waiting for someone to die or grasping at straws. There are certain times when even doctors know that there is a lot more to do beyond the medical model. And of course, in many of the area hospitals, they do a lot of healing too.

BCM: *What else would you like to say about the Center?*

SA:　Well, the Center *is*, as I said, focused on *life*. And even though we deal with issues of death, too, it still is a part of life. People have made friends here. It's a social outlet. Saturday night dinners and entertainment and of course the classes.

BCM: *You feed people in many ways in your Center.*

SA:　Right, that's a good point. We even have a Ph.D. Nutritionist that's here every week who provides counseling. We have a gentleman who has been dealing with insurance benefits and government forms, that type of thing, for years, and he comes in every Saturday and gives counseling individually and will help assist people with benefit problems, like Medicare, Medi-Cal, Social Security, etc. So we really are addressing the spiritual needs, practical needs, emotional needs, psychological needs and physical needs of the person.

BCM: *And you take donations.*

SA: Yeah, everything here at the Center is offered free of charge and people are encouraged, but not expected, to leave something in the basket on their way out. Some can and that's great and appreciated, and some can't, and that's okay, and we still help them. Because we are here to be of service. But of course we wouldn't be here if people weren't supporting us financially. And the miraculous thing is that the community has been supporting us, both financially and through donations of furniture, food; all the things we need for the Center. And the place is really nice looking. It's not castaway stuff that people had, it's really good quality things that people chose to send. So, what else?

BCM: *I don't know if I've asked you this. I asked about your feelings about death. I'm wondering what you would conceive of as an "ideal way to go," or "ideal death."*

SA: Well, I'm just beginning to realize that after all this intense work I've been doing, even though I'm with dying people as a life choice, I'm more alive than I've ever been, and I feel healthier and younger than I've ever felt in my life.

BCM: *Is it because you have let go of so much fear of death?*

SA: I've let go of a lot of fear. Yes. I really believe that. I mean I still have a lot to worry about, a lot more to let go of. There are a lot of neurotic things that go on inside me all the time. But relatively speaking, I'm just so alive now! I feel younger than I've ever felt before in my life. When I was a teenager I was an old man. People who knew me then told me that. I was not a part of this world. And I am now. So I now have this concept of aliveness that has nothing to do with how long I'm going to live. As for the concept of how my own death will be, well, I have speculated on that.

BCM: *Perhaps it's not something we need to dwell on.*

SA: It's not. It's really not. I'm willing to accept it however it comes, but of course I have my own fears about what that scene may look like. All I know is that however I end up coming to terms with it, I hope that it's joyous and miraculous and with loving people around my bedside and that I'm conscious when I go. And not drugged. I want to know when I'm going. I want to experience the transition as it happens. And you know, I've talked to many patients who have had near death experiences at different points of their illness, experiences that were just amazing. Their stories were astounding. I want to be there when it happens. I want to be fully conscious.

BCM: *And that can happen more and more. People have more and more of a say-so. They are demanding a right to die the way they want. The right to be medicated the way they want, or not to be medicated at all, if they want. People are now taking charge of their own lives until the last minute.*

SA: Right. I see it all the time. Especially here. A lot of the people who are coming here are coming because they're not just willing to go with the mainstream all the time. So they know that there are other things they want to complement their medical process. They are taking control of their lives, changing their diets. I don't see any of them doing things that I would say are inappropriate or unhelpful; instead they're incorporating into their lives things that we should all be doing our entire life, like getting the right kind of exercise and rest and nutrition. That's what they're doing, and it's wonderful.

BCM: *So however many years they live on the planet, they will be quality years, loving, joyful and serviceful.*

SA: You got it. And even those that are coming in here while they are ill are also volunteering their time. They are receiving and giving at the same time.

BCM: *That's a very important point that I don't think has been covered before, Stuart. I'm really glad you said that. Because there's always something that we have to give. And so often the person who is ill is in a place where they are experiencing what it feels like to be taken care of or what it is to receive, which is also very difficult for people. As you take charge of your life and your death, you* do *have something to give to others. Just as you receive so from people here at the Center, as a part of your healing, I receive so from Michael and that extends through the veil to the other side.*

SA: And isn't he still giving?

BCM: *Oh, he's giving all the time. He's with me all the time.*

SA: People are always thanking me for what I'm doing here. Some of them just don't realize how much I feel I'm getting. I often feel I'm receiving ten times more than I'm ever giving to this place. I leave here some days and I'm just in awe of what I've gotten here in that one day. Of course there are other days I'm totally wiped out and think at the time that I don't want to be here. But that's just another part of it. My life has changed as a result of being a part of the Center every day. It's just been wonderful.

BCM: *The L.A. Center for Living seems to me like a center of consciousness that reaches out through each indi-*

vidual to touch so many lives. As you continue to evolve and clear your consciousness, then the Center becomes even clearer and more loving. As do, of course, the other people who are involved here, like Marianne and Cassandra, and all the people who drop-in, or volunteer. Then the Center is a collective consciousness of dedicated loving human beings engaged in service.

SA: Yeah, and I want to make that point, even reinforce what you're saying. I know the Center is not me. It may be partially a reflection of my own growth and my own consciousness, but it is such a *collection* of loving consciousness. It attracts people. And it's not me alone or Marianne alone or Cassandra alone, or any of the volunteers alone. I mean, I could leave tomorrow and the Center's energy would still continue. So I don't pretend that I'm any more than a vehicle to help create this collection of loving energy and service.

BCM: *It's like the opposite of, for instance, a certain hospital which might have a very negative atmosphere because of the collective consciousness of the people involved working there and the sadness and grief and rage there of the people who are dying there. Instead, what we feel at the L.A. Center For Living is the collective consciousness evolving with us. We feel that energy growing and expanding, growing out in a very positive way. That sounds like a winner to me, Stuart.*

SA: It is a winner.

The Gift of Caring can be expressed in many ways, whether it is through a Center such as the L.A. Center For Living, the help of a therapist or minister, the kind words of a fellow caregiver, or written materials which boost our spirits when needed.

The following material, distilled from several sources, can be referred to again and again as you move through your own stages of giving care, grieving, and recovering from grief.

"When A Friend Is Dying," and "Saying Goodbye To Someone You Love," will help you and the dying person in your loving attitude towards one another at this critical time.

"How To Take Care Of *You* When You Are Caring For Someone Who Is Critically Ill," offers loving reminders to help you be kind to yourself.

"How To Help A Loved One Through Life's Greatest Challenge," gives ten powerful steps to help you and your loved one through death.

"Symptoms of Loss," "Stepping Stones To Grief Recovery," and "A Minister Looks At Stages Of Loss," will help you throughout your mourning process and grief recovery.

*   *   *

When a Friend is Dying

By Chelsea Psychotherapy Associates:
Dixie Beckham, CSW; Luis Palacios-Jimenez, CSW, ACSW;
Vincent John Patti, CSW; Michael Shernoff, CSW, ACSW.

When someone you know becomes ill, especially with a serious illness like AIDS or cancer, you may feel helpless or inadequate. If this person is a good friend, you may say, "Just call if you need anything." Then out of fear or insecurity, you may dread the call if it comes. Here are some thoughts and suggestions to help you help someone who is ill.

Try not to avoid your friend. Be there; it instills hope. Be the friend, the loved one you've always been, especially now when it is most important.

Touch your friend. A simple squeeze of the hand or a hug can let him or her know that you care.

Call and ask if it is okay to come for a visit. Let your friend make the decision. If he or she may not feel up to visitors that day, you can always visit on another occasion. Now is a time when your friendship can help keep loneliness and fear at a distance.

Respond to your friend's emotions. Weep with your friend when he or she weeps. Laugh when your friend laughs. It's healthy to share these intimate experiences. They enrich you both.

Call and say you would like to bring a favorite dish. Ask what day and time would be best for you to come. Spend time sharing a meal.

Go for a walk or outing together but ask about and know your friend's limitations.

Offer to help answer any correspondence which

may be giving some difficulty or which your friend is avoiding.

Call your friend and find out if anything is needed from the store. Ask for a shopping list and make a delivery to your friend's house.

Celebrate holidays and life with your friend by offering to decorate the home or hospital room. Bring flowers or other special treasures. Include your friend in your holiday festivities. A holiday doesn't have to be marked on a calendar; you can make every day a holiday.

Check in with your friend's spouse, lover, care-partner, roommate, or family member. They may need a break from time to time. Offer to care for your friend in order to give the loved ones some free time. Invite them out. Remember, they may need someone to talk with as well.

Your friend may be a parent. Ask about the children. Offer to bring them to visit.

Be creative. Bring books, periodicals, taped music, a poster for the wall, home-baked cookies or delicacies to share. All of these can bring warmth and joy.

It's okay to ask about the illness, but be sensitive to whether your friend wants to discuss it. You can find out by asking, "Would you like to talk about how you're feeling?" However, don't pressure.

Like everyone else, a person with a serious illness can have both good and bad days. On good days treat your friend as you would any other friend. On the bad days, however, treat your friend with extra care and compassion.

You don't always have to talk. It's okay to sit together silently reading, listening to music, watching television, holding hands. Much can be expressed without words.

Can you take your friend somewhere? Transportation may be needed to a treatment, to the store or bank, to the physician, or perhaps to a movie. How about just a ride to the beach or the park?

Tell your friend how good he or she looks, but only if it is realistic. If your friend's appearance has changed, don't ignore it. Be gentle; yet remember, never lie.

Encourage your friend to make decisions. Illness can cause a loss of control over many aspects of life. Don't deny your friend a chance to make decisions, no matter how simple or silly they may seem to you.

Tell your friend what you'd like to do to help. If your friend agrees to your request, do it. Keep any promises you make.

Be prepared for your friend to get angry with you for no obvious reason, although you feel that you've been there and done everything you could. Remember, anger and frustration are often taken out on the people most loved because it's safe and will be understood.

Gossip can be healthy. Keep your friend up to date on mutual friends and other common interests. Your friend may be tired of talking about symptoms, doctors and treatments.

What's in the news? Discuss current events. Help keep your friend from feeling that the world is passing by.

Offer to do household chores, perhaps taking out the laundry, washing dishes, watering plants, feeding and walking pets. This may be appreciated more than you realize. However, don't do what your friend wants and can do for him or herself. Ask before doing anything.

Send a card that says, simply, "I care!"

If your friend is religious, ask if you could pray together. Spirituality can be very important at this time.

Don't lecture or direct your anger at your friend if he or she seems to be handling the illness in a way that you think is inappropriate. You may not understand what the feelings are and why certain choices are being made.

A loving family member can be a source of strength. Remember that by being a friend or lover you are also a part of the family.

Do not confuse acceptance of the illness with defeat. This acceptance may free your friend and give your friend a sense of his or her own power.

Talk with your friend about the future: tomorrow, next week, next year. It's good to look toward the future without denying the reality of today.

Bring a positive attitude. It's catching.

Finally, take care of yourself! Recognize your own emotions and honor them. Share your grief, anger, feelings of helplessness, or whatever is coming up for you, with others or a support group. Getting the support you need during this crisis will help you to be the real friend for your friend.

*   *   *

Saying Goodbye to Someone You Love

By Chelsea Psychotherapy Associates:
Dixie Beckham, CSW, ACSW; Luis Palacios-Jimenez, CSW;
Vincent John Patti, CSW; Michael Shernoff, CSW, ACSW.

Death is a normal and inevitable part of everyone's life. Yet few of us are prepared to deal effectively with someone who is dying. Very often we are left feeling powerless and helpless. There is a sense that there is little we can do to make a difference during this time.

Everyone dies differently and as they need to. Some people die fighting, others have given up, and still others may die pretending they are not dying. Allow your loved ones to face their final moments as they wish. Remember, there is no right or wrong way to die. Denying one's own death is common. If it doesn't hurt anyone, don't try to take this away from the dying. After all, what have you got to replace the denial with?

Many people die in character, often exactly how they lived. Not everyone can meet death in a noble or heroic way. There is integrity in dying in one's own way.

Understand that your loved one may fear dying, or even welcome it.

Dying can be very different from our expectations. Don't mold the reality of the moment into a romantic idea of what it should be. Despite how difficult it is, be there and remain real.

Dying people still have hope: of not suffering anymore, of being remembered, of an afterlife. Try to support their hope. They may not have anything else at this time.

Someone who is dying may be very angry and striking out inappropriately at those who are closest to him or her. Try not to take this personally.

Though a normal part of life, death can sometimes look, sound and smell ugly. Prepare yourself and move on. Try not to let this interfere with the relationship you have with the person who is dying. Don't let the pain or unpleasantness get in the way of your love and being there.

LOGISTICS

The dying have special needs. Sometimes they need to plan their own funerals or make other arrangements. Inquire about whether you could be helpful in carrying out these last wishes.

Sometimes a dying person needs to give away things that he or she has cherished in the hope of helping keep their memory alive.

RECONCILIATION

What can you do for someone during their last weeks or days, their final moments? Tell them what they mean to you, what you've learned from them. Tell them when you will think about them. Reminisce about the wonderful, funny, or difficult times you shared. Touch and hold them. Understand that all we have between people are moments; moments of loving, of sharing, of being close and understood.

The end of life is a time for reconciliation and closure, for completing unfinished business. Spend time with your friend whether crying, laughing, or silently holding hands. These experiences will provide profound and fresh memories.

It's not unusual to become aware of one's own mortality when someone we love is dying. Death destroys the illusion that we have 'enough time.' Use what time you have left together to affirm you both, to say anything you may or may not have expressed yet.

Our illness or someone else's can make us question

the nature of life. We may become angry at God. It's okay. Remember, God is big enough to survive our anger.

Take stock of spiritual beliefs and reaffirm them. God or whatever deity we may believe in can be a source of comfort, healing and tranquility.

GRIEF

Death is the final part of living. It may be the ultimate life crisis. It requires a special coping and adjusting. Just how do we say "good-bye" to a life of sharing and loving? Although our loved one is physically gone, our feelings don't go with them. This is the nature of grief.

The mourning process often begins at the time of diagnosis and continues long after the person has died.

It is often common for the surviving lover or caregiver to feel relief immediately following the death of a loved one. This is especially likely to be true if the dying process has been drawn out and difficult.

You may not believe death has really happened. Some people experience disbelief and shock.

The absence of grief immediately following the death of a loved one may be a warning sign that you may have a lot of difficulty later on. This may be a form of denial. While we all use denial and it is normal and often useful, we must remember that the pain is still there, even if we're not feeling it.

You may notice others acting inappropriately. Allow them to express their grief in their own way.

Grief is a process of healing that takes time. Learn to nurture yourself. Don't allow the intensity of the pain to frighten you.

The hurt can feel like a bottomless pit, but you do eventually feel better. To hurt from a loss is okay and normal.

You may feel that life isn't worth living without the deceased. This is only a passing feeling, not an answer.

Intense weeping is one of the main expressions of grief. It is often a necessary release of feelings as well as a means of establishing contact with others during these painful moments. Crying can be healthy and cleansing. But not everyone is a crier, so don't try to force this if it is not a natural way for you to react.

While grieving, certain things may occur: shortness of breath, tightness in your throat, frequent sighing, sadness, fatigue, difficulty concentrating, loss of appetite, difficulty sleeping, loss of sex drive, a belief that you're hearing the voice of the deceased.

During this time it's not uncommon for some people to yearn to be reunited with their loved one. You may search for her in a crowded room or on the street; you may expect him to be home waiting for you, or you may call his name at night. You may actually imagine seeing her in places she used to frequent.

If you experience any of the things described in the above two paragraphs, don't become alarmed, many people report that some of these things happen to them following the death of someone they loved.

The traditional rituals of mourning such as wakes, funerals, burials, shiva, memorial services, cemetery stones, novenas, etc., can serve an important function in bringing closure. The ceremonies help make accepting the reality of death easier and provide a structure and form to the grieving process. Don't deprive yourself of them if they are meaningful to you.

Mourning is a way of saying good-bye. Don't avoid it. You need time for healing. Pictures, letters, and other pieces of the deceased's personal property can be helpful during this process. Use them to help get you through this period.

Try to take better care of yourself now more than ever.

After someone's death it's not uncommon to need a vacation, to get away or lie on a beach. Getting some space and distance can be immensely helpful and healing.

Rest and take care of yourself, but beware of isolating yourself from friends, family, and the living. Throughout it all, remember that others can help. This is not a time to feel alone. A friend, family member, social worker, or a clergy person may be useful people to reach out to. Mourning needs resolution in order for you to go on with your life.

The period of mourning immediately following a death is not the time to make any major decisions. Wait. If it is the correct thing to do, time will tell.

You may be very angry without realizing it. Try not to turn the anger or rage against yourself. Let it out. It's okay. A truly horrible thing has just happened to you. The loss of a spouse, lover, child, or close friend is an excellent reason to be angry.

You may be very angry at the deceased for dying. This is normal. Forgiveness plays an important part in grief. You may need to forgive him or her for dying and leaving you. You may need to forgive yourself for all the things you could have done or would have done differently.

Grieving is a process of letting go of what might have been or should have been. It is a time for making peace with the reality of your loss and for saying "good-bye."

A loved one's death can trigger old memories of other losses; a mother, a brother, a divorce, being fired. These memories may make this time even more painful.

Realize you may also be mourning the dreams you had for the deceased. As a spouse, it may be the house you wanted to buy or that special trip you never got to take. As a parent, it may be the hopes you had for your child. It is especially difficult for a parent to have a child die. It is not part of the natural order of things for a parent to bury his or her child.

Birthdays, anniversaries, and holidays following the death of a loved one may be especially painful.

We don't always have control over memories. That special song can reawaken old feelings. Just acknowledge to yourself that although painful this is another normal aspect of grief. Feelings remind us that we are still alive, as well as rekindling memories of our dead loved one.

After the initial shock and disbelief a period of disorganization may happen. The hardest time of all may be long after everyone else is gone. Things are settled down and life returns to what it was before, only your loved one has died. Be aware that the loss is settling in. You may feel empty inside.

You cannot continue to live your life as if the deceased were still alive. This does not mean that you have to give up your loved one. The task is to find ways to let that person live on in your memory.

Try not to worry about "Am I grieving correctly?" You'll do it in your own style and at your own pace. There is no correct way to grieve.

Don't deny your urges to exercise your faith, religion, or spirituality. It may provide some needed answers.

A point of understanding and acceptance eventually occurs. The preoccupation with what has happened and with your dead loved one *does* diminish over time. The intense feelings lessen, and memories become less painful. A renewed interest in other people and in life in general does occur.

It's okay to survive the death of someone you love.

*   *   *

How to Take Care of "You" When You are Caring for Someone Who is Critically Ill

These guidelines are reprinted by permission from "How to Help a Loved One Through Life's Greatest Challenge." by Cassandra Christenson, R.N.

YOU ARE VERY IMPORTANT

Be kind, gentle, and understanding of yourself. Your needs are important. Say what you need to say, don't wait. Appreciate what you are going through and give yourself encouragement.

Be with your loved one for the amount of time comfortable for you and in the way that is natural for you.

Take time out for your feelings. Spend time with yourself. Write, cry, sleep. Take little naps, warm baths, walks, and get hugs. Do nice things for you.

Grief, anger, and other difficult feelings can come at surprising times. And life threatening situations often bring out old memories of sorrow and pain from previous losses. So give yourself the opportunity to sort out these feelings and concerns with a supportive friend or a helping professional.

Being there for the one who is ill is the most important thing you can do. Reevaluate the rest of your activities and do only those which are imperative.

Let people know what you need. Be specific and have the courage to ask and to delegate. Have a friend clean your home, do shopping, do the laundry. Ask the parents of your child's playmate to take your son or daughter under their wing for a special treat.

You may want to call a Hospice Volunteer or others from the community to come in and give you a rest.

Take time for the children in your life, to hug and laugh and cry together. Talk to them and explain in simple language what is happening. Consider their need to play and laugh and understand.

Try not to be intimidated by the hospital environment, the illness itself, and professionals and others who may think they know better how you should be or what you should do.

Forgive yourself! This will be difficult. You will not always know if what you are doing is correct. So be gentle with yourself and forgive yourself for those things which you wish you had said or done differently.

*   *   *

How to Help a Loved One Through Life's Greatest Challenge

These guidelines are reprinted by permission from "How to Help a Loved One Through Life's Greatest Challenge." *by Cassandra Christenson, R.N.*

Help for the one who is ill and for cherished friends and family who wish to be there in the last moments and hours of life.

The following ten steps will help you to be at the bedside with love and tender care so leaving the planet can come in an atmosphere of warmth, safety, and gentle nobility.

1. TRUST YOURSELF. Have the courage to trust your own self and what you wish for the one you love. Your intuition, your open heart, and your own inner guidance will direct you.

2. LET THE ONE YOU LOVE KNOW YOU ARE NOT GOING TO GIVE UP ON HIM OR HER. You are very important. What you have to give at this time of passage is as important as anything the medical profession can give.

3. TOUCH AND BE VERY NEAR. Being sick is a scary time for people and exaggerates feelings of aloneness and isolation. Touching says, "You are not alone, I am with you." Being close and touching are basic ways of showing a person that thay are loved, safe, and cared for. If possible, put the railing of the bed down. Do what has been most natural for you in your relationship.

4. SPEAK DIRECTLY, SIMPLY, AND LOVINGLY. Make your words easy to understand and clear. Look into the eyes of the one who is ill, even if closed or if there is

unconsciousness, as though the eyes are open. Assume you are heard, there is a good chance you are.

5. SAY THE THINGS THAT NEED TO BE SAID. Make peace in the relationship: forgiveness, appreciation, and understanding of the greater purpose of your life together. Share the specific things you love in the other and what his or her life has meant to you. Be gentle, kind, and understanding. The one who is critically ill must feel cherished, honored, and know that his or her life has counted.

6. ACKNOWLEDGE THE NEED FOR SILENCE. Death is deep beyond our understanding. The person who is dying needs time for quiet introspection. Respect this, as you continue to be there with your loving attention and reassuring nearness.

7. BRING BEAUTY, WARMTH, AND LIFE TO THE ROOM. Cherished music, poetry, paintings, flowers from the garden, a blossom pinned to the pillow or taped to the railing of the bed, pets, children, a hand-made cover, a lovely scarf of soft material for about the neck, a favorite article of clothing to be worn.

8. ENCOURAGE A LETTING GO OF THE FEARFUL "HOLDING ON." In this there is less pain and stress, and the body can more easily respond to any medicine or oxygen being given. And if death is to come, it will come with ease and gentle relief.

9. WHEN THE ACTUAL MOMENT OF LEAVING THE PLANET COMES, RESIST THE IMPULSE "TO DO SOMETHING" OR TAKE ACTION. Know this is a precious, holy time, both for you and the one you are with. Continue to be there with your open heart and your loving presence.

10. KNOWING WHAT TO DO AND WHAT TO EXPECT DOES NOT MEAN YOU ARE SURRENDERING TO DEATH. In fact, when it isn't so fearful, it can make you, and the one who is ill, stronger.

THIS CAN BE A GENTLE HAPPENING AND AN EX-
TRAORDINARY AND POSITIVE LIFE EXPERIENCE.
TRUST AND ALLOW IT TO TEACH YOU AND SHOW
YOU THE WAY.

*   *   *

Symptoms of Loss

By Deborah Roth, *The Center For Help in Time of Loss*, From Stepping Stones To Grief Recovery

MOST PEOPLE WHO SUFFER A LOSS EXPERIENCE ONE OR MORE OF THE FOLLOWING:

Feel tightness in the throat or heaviness in the chest.

Have an empty feeling in their stomach and lose their appetite.

Feel restless and look for activity but find it difficult to concentrate.

Feel as though the loss isn't real, that it didn't happen.

Sense the loved one's presence: like finding themselves expecting the person to walk in the door at the usual time; hearing their voice; or seeing their face.

Wander aimlessly and forget or don't finish things they've started to do around the house.

Have difficulty sleeping, and dream of their loved one frequently.

Experience an intense preoccupation with the life of the deceased.

Assume mannerisms or traits of their loved one.

Feel guilty or angry over things that happened or didn't happen in the relationship with the deceased.

Feel intensely angry at the loved one for leaving them.

Feel as though they need to take care of other people who seem uncomfortable around them by politely not talking about their feelings of loss.

Need to tell, retell and remember things about the loved one and the experience of their death.

Feel their mood changes over the slightest things.

Cry at unexpected times.

THESE ARE ALL NATURAL AND NORMAL GRIEF
RESPONSES.

*   *   *

Stepping Stones to Grief Recovery

1. THE DECISION TO ASK FOR HELP
2. THE WILLINGNESS TO SHATTER
3. THE HOPE TO FIND A WAY THROUGH
4. THE HONESTY TO LOOK WITHIN
5. THE PATIENCE TO STICK WITH THE PROCESS
6. THE TRUST TO KEEP OPEN
7. THE GRATITUDE TO PASS IT ON

Deborah Roth
The Center For Help in Time of Loss
From *Stepping Stones To Grief Recovery*

A Minister Looks at Stages of Loss

By Margie Ann Nicola, Assistant Minister,
Unity-By-The-Sea

As I observe those who are "left behind" there is a recognizable evolution of grief. Below, I outline some of the stages of grief many people experience, and include suggestions for coping with these feelings.

DENIAL OF LOSS. "I should not grieve for God needs them more than I; They've gone on to their good so I'm okay; We were together for so many years, I must be grateful for what I had; I'm just feeling sorry for myself if I feel bad," and on and on.

When we love, we may experience loss. The pain of loss is a real and powerful experience. Grieving is necessary. To reenter the mainstream of life, we must allow ourselves to feel the feelings so that we can release them. The pain of loss is normal and natural.

GUILT OVER UNFINISHED BUSINESS. "If I could have just said I was sorry; If they would have forgiven me; I should have visited more; I should have been more loving."

Because I believe death is merely moving into another dimension of living, I encourage those left behind to write a letter to the friend or loved one who has just died; or, in their mind, express the feelings and say the words that were not shared. I believe that in God there is no time and space, therefore the words and feelings are received and a healing takes place.

GUILT FOR FEELING "THEY FINALLY DIED." There may even be a sense of relief. This is usually experienced following a long illness that has placed stress on the family left behind. Or, perhaps the deceased was a controller and had made the bereaved's life miserable.

If we will deal with our feelings honestly rather than burying or denying them, we will move through them faster with less pain.

ANGER WITH THE PERSON FOR DYING. Usually in the case of a spouse or parent. There is a sense of betrayal and abandonment. This is a natural reaction to the loss.

Again, if we do not fight or deny this feeling, it will pass. The anger is a result of fear. Involvement in *life* will alleviate the fear and anger.

DEPRESSION. This can follow any of the previous stages. Often it occurs because the bereaved stops in the middle of a process and does not move on through to their next step in grieving and returning to life.

Seek professional and spiritual help. The longer we allow ourselves to be depressed, the more difficult it is to release it. Depression is a result of immobility of thought and activity. Find something in life to capture your mind and imagination.

THE SENSE OF LOSS. This is a natural, normal emotional separation. This stage may encompass some or all of the above stages. Allow emotions to surface and then move on through the experience. Accept the pain and know that the pain will diminish and recede.

A belief system that provides a strong foundation, a comforting reassurance that all is well in spite of the loss, creates the space in which we can allow ourselves to understand that pain and loss are a part of living. We are more than our pain and more than our loss.

ANNIVERSARIES. Grief resurfaces on the anniversaries of the death, special events that had been shared such as family gatherings, etc.

Again, rather than withdrawing from the experience, participate both in the event and the remembrance. All is well and very normal and natural.

As a counselor, I see my function as recognizing which stage of grief the counselee is in and assisting them to move through the process and reenter their every day activities as quickly and as easily as possible. Compassion rather than sympathy, encouragement rather than commiserating, seems to be the best support I can offer.

I say to each person grieving, when you add up all your experiences of life, even the painful ones, they have created the opportunity for you to become strong in mind and forced you to seek higher wisdom and guidance.

In spite of every wound you have been dealt, you have not been destroyed and the pain experienced may have been the driving force for you to turn to a higher power.

Until we give up our belief that pain will kill us, and allow ourselves to go *through* the pain, we will never face the past, forgive it, accept it, and love it. The past represents Life and we cannot deny Life and expect to enjoy what Life has to give to us.

The Gift
of
Unconditional
Love

This is what death should be; a quiet choice,
made joyfully and with a sense of peace, because
the body has been kindly used to help the Son of
God along the way he goes to God. We thank the
body, then, for all the service it has given us. But
we are thankful, too, the need is done to walk the
world of limits, and to reach the Christ in hidden
form and clearly seen at most in lovely flashes.
Now we can behold Him without blinders, in the
light that we have earned to look upon again.

— Song of Prayer
A Course In Miracles
Foundation For Inner Peace

8

Marianne Williamson is a minister and a well-known spiritual teacher in Los Angeles who lectures extensively on *A Course in Miracles* (a three-volume set of spiritual teachings on unconditional love) all over the country. She is founder of The Los Angeles Center For Living, a loving place where people with terminal illnesses, their families and friends, *and* professional caregivers come together to assist one another through the dying experience with unconditional love. Marianne is also writing a book tentatively titled *Conscious Contact: The Power of Surrender*.

I interviewed Marianne at her home in West Hollywood, just a few blocks from the Los Angeles Center For Living. She is a young, vibrant, slender woman who crackles with intensity. As we talked, we found that we are aligned in vision, clarity of purpose and in our own personal sense of service.

What follows is an intense expression of Marianne's beliefs on unconditional love and service as realized through her life and teaching and her current work with the Los Angeles Center For Living.

BCM: *The gift I'd like to focus on is the gift of unconditional love, and how you, Marianne, as a spiritual teacher, apply that gift in your work. From this gift of uncondi-*

tional love, I want to know a little bit about the steps that led you, first into teaching A Course in Miracles *and becoming so well known in that arena, and then secondly, to founding the Los Angeles Center For Living.*

MW: In my view of the world, we're all here for the same purpose. And that's to heal the planet. And we all have different gifts. But what *A Course in Miracles* talks about is how we're all here to be ministers of God. We're all here to open our hearts and to forgive and to heal the bleeding heart. So, *you* do that through writing, *I* do it through teaching. It's the same work. Because you're teaching, and I'm teaching; it doesn't matter if it's oral or it's written. So the first place I'm coming from, is just from a sense of devotion. And what AIDS does is bring into very clear focus, through an apparent crisis, how much we need to be devoted to the healing of the earth. AIDS is like a festering sore, but the dis-ease in humanity has been there for a long time. What AIDS represents for me is one more opportunity where I feel that the open heart is saying, "What can I do?" That to me is a real deepening of the spiritual life. Not just opening your heart, but following the compassion that flows into your heart with, "What can I do?" Eight years ago, I went through a private grief and was very aware that there was no place for me to go. Once a week I had an appointment with a psychiatrist. What was I supposed to do in between?

BCM: *Tell me about it!*

MW: You've told your friends so much, that you cannot bear to lay it on them one more time. They've been wonderful, but four or five months later, *they're* ready to move on, *you* still have processing to do. And I remember thinking that if I ever got through this, other people would have an easier time of it than I did from what I had learned. First of all, I think grief, as you well know, is a very transformative experience. I say to people all the time, "Definitely, you will not be the same person on the other side of this. Your only choice is whether you will be harder or softer." *Grief breaks your heart.* So on the other side of that you will either close down or you will open up beyond any opening you've ever had before. Now, when you open your heart you open to God. And in *A Course in Miracles* it says, "As you grow closer to God you grow closer to your natural talent of protecting your brothers." Really living close to God moves you closer to others. I remember when I went through my grief, and you might relate to this, I remember looking around at humankind and thinking, "Do any of these people hurt like this?" Because if they have hurt a *fraction* of the amount that I'm hurting right now, I feel so sorry for them.

BCM: *And how can they be walking around when you hurt so bad you can't hardly draw a breath?*

MW: *How* can they be walking around? What I got back in response, from my own internal wisdom was this: they *do* suffer, they *have* been suffering, you just never noticed. See, they're looking at *you* and they don't know. Assume it. Assume it. Because even if they're not suffering big, we all have our little griefs on a daily basis. And my heart opened from that. And from my own grief, from my own heartbreak, I finally began to understand that the resurrection, the victory, is that something good is going to come out of this.

BCM: *Oh, yes!*

MW: I know you know.

BCM: *Yes, I do.*

MW: And that gives you a *fierce power*. That gives you a fierce power. It gives you a vision, it gives you a clarity, it gives you a dynamism, and things happen because of it. So much like you, Betty-Clare, my work is very the same. And out of my grief came my ministry, and to me, the Los Angeles Center For Living was an extension of that. There were a couple of aspects that interested me concerning the Center. First of all, it's part of my work. What I'm interested in is changing the world. The transformation of our world. And I know that our institutions will change because we change.

BCM: *Why not go for the highest dream, the big picture.*

MW: Yes. Go for the best.

BCM: *Change the world.*

MW: Yes. And this city, Los Angeles, is a place where, well, there is *no* context that I know of where we have as much permission, emotionally and psychologically, to do whatever we need to do to change ourselves if we want to. And from that changed perspective we assist in transforming the planet.

It's interesting that there is actually a positive side to the current political climate and the social service cutbacks. I do not, and never will, agree to what I see as a kind of mean-spiritedness to current Washington politics, but at least it's become very clear to me that if social good is going to exist, *we* are going to have to pay for it.

BCM: *Nobody's going to do it up in Washington.*

MW: No, nobody's going to do it. Nobody's going to pay for it. If you want it, *you* do it. That became clear to me in the midst of the AIDS crisis, and not just AIDS actually. . .

BCM: *Dead is dead. Whether it's AIDS or something else. We realize that there are some especially heart-wrenching challenges for those of us who see someone young die before their time, which forces us to face our own beliefs about life and death and a merciful God. But at the same time I want to reiterate to you that this book will be for* everyone *who is dealing with the death process.*

MW: I understand. The initial impetus for the Center came because of a girlfriend of mine who had cancer. Breast cancer. When she was first diagnosed, she had done all of the holistic things to do. Two years later, the doctor told her she had maybe six months to live, and she said to me when we were having lunch one day, "For two years I've looked for someone to help me heal; now I wish there was someone I could go to to help me die." And when she said that, the room began spinning for me. Goose bumps. And I *knew* that was a call to me. I went home and I called several people that I know that are involved professionally on a daily basis with these issues, and I said, "Will you join with me? Would you be interested in supporting people through the issues around death?" I became very interested in hospice philosophy at that time. Now, as you well know, my concern is that there is kind of a metaphysical half-truth out there—"you can heal yourself"—that has some people finding that they're doing all their spiritual homework, and yet they're still dying, and so now on top of everything else, they can beat themselves up with their spiritual failure.

BCM: *This is something I address to audiences all the time. I speak across the country, because I was co-founder of Mothers of AIDS Patients, and I do a lot of speaking with my books. This was a hard truth for me to learn because I had been a metaphysician for years. But my son and I learned together that healing doesn't mean healing of the physical body.*

MW: Not at all!

BCM: *It means healing the heart.*

MW: Finding peace.

BCM: *The acceptance of surrender. And I speak vehemently on this very issue because my son on his deathbed was saying, ''Mother, I feel like I'm a spiritual failure because I didn't think myself well,'' and I'm here to inveigle against that whole ''metaphysical blackmail'' syndrome.*

MW: Me too! Me too. That was my point exactly. *A Course in Miracles* says that healing is a return to inner peace. And sometimes the form of the healing is death. We have a judgement that life should be longer. So that is exactly my point. And I said, "all I want is to have a place where death, the word death, can come out of the closet." When Jesus said, "Death will be the last enemy," what he meant is it's the last thing you'll *perceive* as an enemy. Death itself is not an enemy. It's just a shedding of clothes and going on towards greater life. That was the point here. I wanted to start a place where it's okay to die.

BCM: *Yes!*

MW: I didn't want to start a place where everybody was going to say, "You can heal, man, you can get your body well." I wanted to start a place where people will love, and whatever form that love takes going, coming, is okay. That was what I wanted. And really, it seemed to me that we had a lot of resources set up, in this town and elsewhere, to help people heal their bodies. What we needed was a place where it's okay if you die too.

BCM: *You are saying exactly what I want heard loud and clear through my work and through this book.*

MW: Good. And I wanted it heard loud and clear through starting the Center. So we're on the exact same wavelength. And that's what I wanted. In fact, it was a challenge for me when the board wanted to call it the Los Angeles Center For Living, because I wanted to call it something like the Center For Death And Dying. When I put it out to the community what I wanted this place for, I told it as it is. I said, "This is a place where we can deal with the subject of death." I really wanted a hospice. We didn't raise enough money for it. But I talked to my friend Gerald Jampolsky who said to me, "Don't be so attached to the idea of a bedded facility." He said, "You can do a lot without it." And I'm sure it's as it should be. Interestingly enough though, even though people responded to that call, the classes specifically having to do with death and dying are not well attended.

BCM: *Yet.*

MW: Yet. Good. Absolutely. In other words, people are open enough that they'll give the money because they know the need is there, but not open enough to go there, but that's okay. The fact that it's there is enough. We're going to have it there, and when you're ready you come. The issue is that the human vehicle responds miraculously and powerfully in the presence of love. It shuts down into smallness in the presence of fear. In our culture we have a major awkwardness around death. I was raised Jewish. In my experience, I've noticed that the Catholics and the Jews know what to do when someone dies, and sometimes the Protestants just stand there and don't know what to do.

BCM: *And close the heart. Because what you do is become a stoic.*

MW: What's interesting though, is that Catholicism and Judaism are really ancient religions. Not ancient, but old religions, much older. So the ritual is much more psychologically based. The reason Catholics and Jews know what to do is because there are these traditions that have been around for thousands of years that *tell* you what to do. The women cook. The men pray. It's like a ritual that you're taught from the time you're children. You get into gear. No one has ever told the Protestants *what to do*. That's why the Jewish people know how to handle it, because someone has told them *what to do*. Not as in what you and I would think of as enlightened things like holding a hand, but at least, get off your rear and *do* something around death. And I noticed that Catholics have a whole tradition of ritual, but Protestants barely have anything. I know in my own life, the fact that I grew up in a Jewish family, I saw my parents get into gear when someone died. Right? I saw them *do* something. And Catholics are the same way. So I saw a lot of people around me with AIDS and cancer and other diseases shut down simply because they didn't know what to do. And so they retreated.

BCM: *And because we are so afraid of death.*

MW: So afraid. Exactly. So the idea is to know that if you step forward in love, this can be embraced. And that to me, that's why I give so many lectures about embracing death. I just felt God saying, "Do something." I felt like you always have to look and see what you can do. It's like the serenity prayer in Alcoholics Anonymous, "Let me make the distinction between what I can change and what I can't change." What I *can't* change is that people are dying. What I sure *can* change, and what is criminal if I *don't* change, is that there are these people, at home, alone, with no one to talk to, no one to take care of them, no one to love them. *That* is something we can do something about. It's my spiritual and professional conviction that when you're part of the solution, you don't feel the same despair. I know you know that. People who are just focusing on the problem rather than the answer are then in despair. So be part of the vibration of the answer!

Death only has victory over you if it causes you to shut down. That's the death. Death can be an opening into greater life if it opens your heart. Then you see that there is no death, because the more you allow your heart to be open the more you know God goes with you. But if you shut your heart down into your grief, then you're affirming that God, and your loved one, are not with you.

BCM: *My heart* can't *shut down anymore!*

MW: Death is not more powerful than the love of God. But you have to choose which master you serve.

BCM: *(softly) Yes. Yes.*

MW: You know, it's interesting. I do a grief group at the Center and there's a woman in it who's son had died, and she said to me, "I was so involved with the Names Project Quilt, and now that it's finished, I'm let down." I said to her, "You were working with spirit while working on the quilt, because you were working with the manifestation of love."

BCM: *Right. just like with the bracelet project. (The Mothers of AIDS Patients PWA national bracelet project honoring those who have died of AIDS. -ed.)*

MW: Exactly. *DO* something! I said to her, "*There is no more powerful force in the universe than a mother's love.*" The whole survival of the species is based on it. Women want to mother. And they have a fierce protection and love for their child, without which babies would die. There is *nothing* like a mother's love. And when a mother's love is turned to the fierce power of conviction, there is nothing that they can't do. My work at the Center is based on the same fierce power of conviction.

BCM: *I wanted to know how the Los Angeles Center For Living serves the community, and you've already answered that in some ways, but I would like to hear your vision of its purpose both now and in the future.*

MW: I felt that God wanted it to be there. What happens now is not my business. What is important is not the Los Angeles Center For Living. What is important is the love that people feel. Whether it's the Los Angeles Center For Living or whether it's some other form, it's just that you're lighting a candle. People can come and get free counseling, ministerial assistance, support groups, bodywork. It's a place where people who have something to give and people who have genuine needs can come and gather. What form it takes matters very little. I have very loose reins with it. It has a life of its own. Stuart Altschuler, the executive director of the Center, reports to me on a weekly basis. I'll tell him if something doesn't feel right, but it's not for me to interfere with its natural evolvement. I listen, I'll tell him, "I'd like to see this," but the Center has got its own life. Something like that is like a child. You don't want to control them and dominate them. They have a life of their own and you just want to very loosely guide.

BCM: *It's an organic thing.*

MW: It's an organic process. Exactly. It's a loving space, and my job, I feel, is merely to protect the energy of the devotional mentality that gave it birth. That's my function work-wise. If you keep the God alignment, that we are doing these things for God, and help people develop a sense of gratitude and devotion, everything else takes care of itself.

BCM: *Yes. Emmet Fox, a wise spiritual teacher, said that an organization is only as good as the consciousness of the person who is directing it or running it.*

MW: Absolutely. Because if I begin trying to *make* the Los Angeles Center For Living be anything specific, then you're back to the control orientation which was the problem to begin with. You know, you're just asking, aren't you, that the Holy Spirit sort of speak brightly through you and through me?

BCM: *Yes, in fact I don't have too much choice over it all! I get fatigued at times because there's always another project down the line and each one is needed.*

MW: Mmm hmm—the future. *A Course in Miracles* teaches us to live in the present. I have been very clear in my work that I'm not indispensible, and neither is any particular form of my work, like the Center. If it's meant to have life, people will continue to fund it, the money will come, and it will *be there*. There are times when I walk into the Center, and I see some boy with lesions whose afternoon is sweeter because the Center is there, and that's all I care about. It doesn't have to be anything grandiose or fancy. I'm very adamant about that and I make it clear with Stewart. It's not about grandiosity. It's just about the simplicity of devotion to the children of God on a moment by moment basis.

BCM: *I love the phrase "simplicity of devotion," because what I've found among caregivers is that when we lay aside our ego and just go for the service, it all happens, but nothing is grandiose. It is a simple devotion of God.*

MW: Absolutely. It's become a little bit chic these days to be involved in some of this stuff and you know the ego loves to corrupt anything, and I just realize that the real power is very simple and devotional, moment by moment. Some woman with cancer gets a facial, some man with AIDS takes a class on Yoga breathing, a family gathers in a grief group.

BCM: *Yes! And feels loved.*

MW: Right.

BCM: *What are your own feelings about death and loss, and how have they changed over the years?*

MW: Like most people that I talk to, I don't have much of a problem anymore with death. But I'd be lying if I said I didn't have a problem with dying.

BCM: *Me too. (Laughter).*

MW: I really do believe what *A Course in Miracles* tells me. I really do believe that there *is* no death. That there is only eternal life. That the body is merely a suit of clothes. And that consciousness remains alive. However, having to get on an airplane after having an experience where a wing caught on fire, it was made very clear to me that when it came down to my *own* mortality, like getting on a plane again when I was scared, I was not nearly as enlightened as I might have thought. (Laughter).

BCM: *Isn't that how it happens to us! It happens to me all the time, Marianne.*

MW: But I had a healing with the airplane business. What happened was that a wing caught on fire over the Pacific and we had to go back to Hawaii. *Just* at that time, very shortly after that, I began having to fly constantly—sometimes twice a week. I still go to New York every other week.

BCM: *I wasn't aware of that.*

MW: I was terrified.

BCM: *I'll bet.*

MW: Because of this experience. And my therapist and my boyfriend at the time kept trying to help me. I remember my boyfriend saying, "You're not going to get over this terror by my telling you that the chances of your dying are not great. You're only going to get over this terror when you really embrace that it doesn't matter if you die." And my therapist said basically the same thing. She said,

"What does it matter, Marianne? You're as dead now as you'll ever be." I have been through a tremendous healing, and I can get on a plane fine, and I don't think that the peace I've achieved comes from thinking, "Oh, it probably won't crash." The peace that I've achieved comes from knowing it really doesn't matter if it does. This is not a statement of where I totally am, but I'm moving towards there.

BCM: *The fire gets hotter. You're working with death, so the fire gets hotter. You get the tests that come into your life, so that you can see where you are.*

MW: I believe that death can be a joyous experience. In Japan, they mourn when someone's born and celebrate when they die. I just have this strong sense that it can be just this amazing openness into light. I'm dedicated to that somehow. I think it can be an exciting experience. We can evolve to the point where it would be.

BCM: *I agree with you about death. I am still learning to heal the agony of the dying process itself when it is long and drawn out and excruciating and doesn't look like all the pretty pictures that we hope for.*

MW: What do you think about that, BettyClare? What is death to you?

BCM: *I think death is a kind friend...*

MW: But sickness is not.

BCM: *...but that the dying process tests us to the limit of our ability to love and that it is the most intense experience that we will ever encounter as we are with someone who is going through that process. Especially someone who is a part of our body, someone we have given birth to. Being there at their birth and their death. And I still have a long way to go to erase some of the horrifying memories that did go along with the* intensity, with the luminous memories, the moments of joy in the midst of despair. And I don't think I can ignore the agony and only remember the intimacy.

MW: You're not supposed to. I do, though, want to remind you that there is a lesson in *A Course in Miracles* which is a line that's in the Bible a lot and that is the lesson that says, "And God himself shall wipe away our tears." And I just support you in that. I certainly don't mean in any way that I think that the answer is for us to stuff our emotions. I understand what you're saying.

BCM: *I had to cut the umbilical cord in meditation before Michael died.*

MW: Or you would have died too.

BCM: *It was in some unconscious way holding him, although I had released him a thousand times to his dear great-grandmother and my grandson who had died. We had done everything right and yet there was still the agony that was going on. And when I forget and get immersed in how I'm going to pay the rent or how many books I'm going to sell or "look how good I learned how to do all this work I do," then there comes an opportunity always to be brought up short and get back to what I'm really here for.*

MW: Me too.

BCM: *And I went to the Names Quilt and wrote, after an incredible night of mourning, "Michael, I will continue your dream." Because this is one thing that I've seen with caregivers. We get to a point of burnout. That's the only word I know for it. And I want this book to recognize that and to assist those of us who are "in the fire" so to speak—Ram Dass' expression just keeps coming to me—to get past that point to the next step. And I am just learning. Every day. So. Do you have anything else at this time to say about this aspect?*

MW: Well you asked me about death and about loss, and I think that basically what you said is the truth. Death is one thing, loss is another. One is kind of an objective experience and principle which is that there is no death. The other is loss which has to do with human emotion. My astrological sign is Cancer. So I turn everybody into a motherly connection. I grieve over the end of relationships when someone is just on the other side of town and doesn't want to talk to me. Amazingly. It seems to be one of my karmic lessons as well, obviously, as yours, to learn to let go with love knowing that as we let go we find that there is in fact no loss, that they're still with us. That's the only thing that I know of that has helped me survive through my experiences of loss. I just know that if we don't go through these things *alone*, we can make it.

BCM: *Yes. Yes.*

MW: And I do believe that one day it will all be like the last scene in "Places in the Heart." Did you see that movie?

BCM: *Three times! The communion. The peace of God.*

MW: I know it.

BCM: *That touched me greatly.*

MW: And once again, why am I here? I'm here to look for that.

A Course in Miracles says, "Remember who walks with you. And if you forget, remind yourself a thousand times a day. And if you forget, remind yourself a thousand times a minute. To know that when you stand in love you literally carry the presence of God with you."

BCM: *I love that. Stand in love.*

MW: And when you feel like, "What can I do?" just know that your showing up and holding love in your mind means you are bringing the power of God. You are affecting the forces of comfort on an invisible level. God will do his part if you'll do yours. If you will just show up, He will tell you what to say, what to do, perhaps just sit there. You will become transformed through an attitude of service. Just don't run away. The *only* enemy is your tendency to want to shut down and run away. The only thing to fear is the fear itself. Just stand forth and ask God continually: "Open my heart and we'll do everything right."

BCM: *That's important. I love to be reminded of this because there are times when I want to run away from the task.*

MW: And sometimes I think people like you and me have seen our love turn into manifestation in the world. We have already gotten to the point where even in our dark moments we have *seen*, we have a conviction born of the fact that we've been doing it long enough, practicing it long enough that we've *seen* effectiveness in the world.

BCM: *(Enthusiastically) Yes. It works! We know God works.*

MW: Other people haven't seen it yet. They may believe it but they haven't seen it yet and they might think, "I'm not even doing anything." If you're standing there, you are there for the dying. You *are* doing it. Just by being there. That's what the caregiver needs to know. Just don't walk out of the room.

BCM: *Right.*

MW: Go into the room where you are needed. I remember my sister used to teach autistic children.
I was with her one day when I was much younger and this one little boy was so autistic, it was
so horrible, and I ran into the bathroom and I was
crying, and she came in and she shook me by the
shoulders and she said angrily, "He doesn't need
your pity! He needs your help."

BCM: *How wonderful.*

MW: And that's what I see. A lot of people patronize
the sick, pity the sick. They don't need your pity,
thank you. They *could* use a trip to the grocery
store, someone who'd be willing to clean their
bedroom, someone who'd be willing to visit. A
friend of mine, Norman, who took care of a
dying loved one was sharing just the other day
about how many people in those last stages
would say, "Norman, what can I do?" And Norman would say, "You could go visit, you know,
he can't get out of the house but you could go
visit him." And everyone kept saying, "What can
I do?" but didn't go to visit!!

And I've joked with people and said, "I was so
bad with situations like that, there was a time
when I could tell you the merchandise in every
hospital gift shop in town." Because I would go to
the hospital, and I didn't want to go up to the
room and I'd stay in the gift shop! (Slowly,
deliberately) GO INTO THE ROOM. Love casts
out fear. It's not about *you*. It's about being there
for *them*. Just show up. And also, the other thing
I would say is that I feel that we are the parental
generation. You shouldn't feel biologically that

you have to have children in order to know that it's your function on this earth to take care of the children.

BCM: *We are nurturers.*

MW: Yes. And by the same token, you shouldn't have to have someone close to you dying to know that it is our mission as human beings to take care of the dying. That must be a consciousness that permeates. You know, it's like that wonderful man who is Surgeon General of the United States, Everett Koop.

BCM: *Yes! Who puts his job and his reputation on the line every day.*

MW: Oh he's so wonderful! And when I saw him on television he was saying, "These people must not be forgotten." It is your mission as a human being to open your heart. And I do believe that those of us who help people die, when our time comes they will be standing at the gate for us to help us.

BCM: *Absolutely. And I really respond to healing your own fear of death because I have seen this as the big resistance behind all the little resistances.*

MW: The last enemy.

BCM: *Yes. The closer we get the more transparent and translucent the veil becomes. When we're dealing with the dying on a daily basis, when we're immersed in this work, there isn't anything between us and death. We have to face it. And when I wrote* When Someone You Love Has AIDS, *I was very fearful when I was going through all these challenges, because I was starting over and I kept saying, "Fear forward. Fear forward. Fear forward." You have to go through that. That tunnel. Literally. In order to be alive.*

MW: And you are alive in a way that you were not alive before this happened.

BCM: *That's true.*

MW: When someone you love is dying, your heart is ripped open. That can actually be a great initiation.

BCM: *You are right. I thought I knew how to love. But I have learned how little I knew and how much more I can love.*

MW: It's easy to love when everyone's doing what you want them to do and need them to do.

BCM: *Oh yes. But when I had people that I love die, it presented one opportunity after another to ask myself, "What do I really believe in? Do I really believe I can get through this, that I can overcome fear with love, or not?"*

MW: Also, one of the things I say to people all the time is, as we both know, when you have suffered, it gives you an x-ray vision into other people's suffering. And then your compassion for people has a special feeling behind it. When I put my hand on somebody's hand and say, "I'm sorry," there's something about the fact that I've felt it too.

BCM: *You feel the difference.*

MW: You feel it. Somebody knows. It makes us healers.

BCM: *Everything that you're saying leads us to the gift that we give which IS that unconditional love.*

MW: That's all. And that's part of what you learn as you walk through the fire. Why do you walk through fire? Because when you put metal into fire it turns into gold. Because the only thing that can burn up is what was never real anyway. That's all that can burn. That's what it means to burn karma. So what happens after you walk through a fire is that everything that was real stands forth and everything else has fallen away.

BCM: *Yes.*

MW: Love was the bottom line before AIDS. AIDS just shows you. Death has a way of showing you. I always say to people, when you've been diagnosed with a potentially life-threatening illness, you drop a lot of garbage in the first thirty seconds. You get really clear really fast what matters and what doesn't. The rest just drops away.

BCM: *Marianne, I find myself very impatient with super-ficialities and superficial people. That sounds like a judgement. I'm really working on my judgments. However, there isn't time for all the everyday garbage, the trivialities, the game playing. When someone you love is dying, all that stuff is useless. It's useless!*

MW: Wasn't there a time, though, when you and I didn't know that?

BCM: *Yes.*

MW: That's my answer to that one. I didn't always know that myself. It's an important point. You and I have a fierceness, a clarity, the power of the "NOW." The time is at hand. But we are all still learning. When you haven't been through these things, you need patience and understanding. In fact, we *all* need patience and understanding. It's like some people don't see purple. They just haven't seen purple so you can't expect them to perceive purple. They're color blind.

BCM: *Right. That's true. That's true. What is your definition of unconditional love?*

MW: Total acceptance. The uprising of the ego mind is to try to resist what is. And to me the presence of love is to embrace what is. Knowing that in the presence of love is the transformation to a different experience. That's why death to me has such a sting, but our *victory* over death is accepting that it might be transformative to a different kind of experience. That's where it's important that we recognize the difference between acceptance and resignation. When I say to people, "Accept the possibility of death," they sometimes get scared. And the truth to me is that if you *deny* the possibility of death, you may just bring it to you, because you still have an unconscious desire to learn and to transform the fear.

BCM: *But you're fighting against it. Michael had to learn to move from control to acceptance. From fighting the illness to just absolute total surrender into God's arms, and I had to move through it with him far beyond lip service. To experience the acceptance myself.*

MW: To soften around the pain, to surrender into it. When I was leaving a two-year relationship, which is nothing compared to losing a child, it was the same type of thing. I didn't want it the way it was. I didn't want it to end. But the lesson for me was that I had no choice, this was not something that I could control, I couldn't get my way, and it was just one more deepening in my life. To accept my peace into God. When I stopped fighting it, I began to accept what was and surrender into what was. To allow it to be. And it's very clear that this is the only reason we're on this earth. Because as we surrender deeper and deeper it's like the skins of an onion. We're becoming the person God really needs us to be. And that's the only reason our souls meet to begin with. Michael was here on this earth to help you become more of what you wanted to be, just as you were there for him.

BCM: *Absolutely. I absolutely agree. This is perfect. (Sounds of hugging, appreciation for one another). Do you have anything else that you'd like to say?*

MW: The only thing I'd like to say is that I think that wonderful things are happening. For all the despair that we could focus on, I see little acts of courage. I see those little miracles all the time. At the Los Angeles Center for Living, I see people working from the best which is within them. That's happening all over the city, and all over the country. Death is just one more opportunity. This generation hasn't grown up, and those of us that are allowing our hearts to be pierced by these kinds of events are growing into real men, real women.

BCM: *Death forces you to be a grown-up.*

MW: It does. It does. And I see a lot of people who are grown up, and are growing up, and I think that, if there's anything that I'd like to say, it's that when you are in the middle of the fire, that's when you begin to see God. When this society begins to transform our perceptions of death it'll be such an amazing evolutionary leap.

BCM: *That's when the last enemy will be overcome as we transform our fear of death.*

MW: See it for what it is. Just a lie. I mean if everybody on this earth consciously agreed with you that Michael is not dead...

BCM: *Oh, he's closer to me now than he ever was. Each time I talk with someone who is working as you are and I am, I am reminded of him. And then little chunks of loss fall away from me. I keep healing. I thank God every night that Michael is with me and we are closer than we ever were when he was a little boy, or a rebellious teenager who ran away, or a grown man living far away from me. His death was an opportunity for us to learn to express our love for one another and I thank God every day for that.*

MW: Everything that happens, happens in order that we may learn to love one another, to love one another unconditionally. Even death. That's the gift. That's the true gift.

The Gift
of
Transformation

PRAYER FOR OPENING THE HEART CENTER

Open my heart, Lord,
That I may see
Visions of good you have for me.

Open my heart, Lord,
That I may hear
Your love and wisdom guiding me clearly.

Open my heart, Lord
That I may feel
All that is true, and all that is real.

Open my heart, Lord,
That I may know
What I must do, and where I must go.

Open my heart, Lord,
That I may be
Whatever, in LOVE, you want me to be.

Open my heart, Lord!

—BettyClare Moffatt

9

The Reverend John-Alexis Viereck, a noted worker in World Peace, is the Spiritual Resource Advisor for the Episcopal AIDS Ministry at St. Augustine By-The-Sea Episcopal Church. He and his wife Mary, are also Psychosynthesis Therapists. Their Chapel of St. John offers private and group spiritual and psychosynthesis counseling.

This Spiritual Rule for Caregivers was developed as a guideline for clergy and therapists working with the dying. It is a remarkable rule for living in the midst of dying. It is a spiritual, meditative discipline, designed to assist, first, the caregiver, and secondly, the dying person making his transition.

It is also used in group meditative work.

While written from an Episcopalian Minister's point of view, this spiritual rule is designed to help people of all faiths.

Some of the terms used within this material may seem unfamiliar at first. However, the rewards of mastering the spiritual rule presented here are incalculable. I use this spiritual rule as a part of my own daily discipline. It can greatly assist the caregiver to continue in his or her work with the dying.

A Spiritual Rule for Death and Dying Ministry and Caregiver Teams

In Luke 9:25, we read, " What will a person gain by winning the whole world at the cost of their true self?"

All spiritual traditions have at their heart the finding and identifying with this True Self or soul. In coming to know or recollect our True Self, we will come to know our life purpose as well. And whatever form it may take, our life purpose is intimately connected with loving, and inseparable from serving. For there where our heart is our treasure will be also.

We have been given an explicit mandate to love one another unconditionally even as we are unconditionally loved. We believe we love God in loving one another. The two cannot be separated. In feeding the hungry, clothing the naked, setting free those who are enslaved, opening the eyes of those who can't see, taking care of the ill, assisting the dying, even as we do this for each of them, we are doing this for God.

The finding of our True Self, coming to know and fulfill our life purpose, and loving and serving God through loving and serving one another and the world are inseparable from spiritual development. This process begins with coming to know, and make conscious contact with, our True Self. For our life on earth is a field of service for the Soul, and our mind and thoughts, our emotions and feelings, and our body and actions—what we call our personal self or ego—do not in fact have a separate life of their own, but are the instruments of the True Self's service. We therefore need to learn to disidentify from them, so as to identify and make conscious connection with our True Self. (The True Self is traditionally described as the experience of at-onement, while the ego is traditionally said to be the source of "sin," or separation from God). To establish right relationship between our True Self or Soul and our personal self or ego and its component parts is the work of all spiritual psychology.

Dr. Roberto Assagioli, the founder of Psychosynthesis, has stated, "We are dominated by everything with which our self becomes identified. We can dominate and control everything from which we disidentify ourselves."

For instance, when we identify with our emotions, and forget that they are a vehicle, a channel or medium to express through, and imagine they are our self, that we *are* our feelings, we become controlled by the life of our emotions, and the nature and limitations of emotional life become the nature and limitations of our whole life. We are no longer masters of our own house. We become attached, we hook in, we react, we swing from one state to another, because that is the nature of emotions, that is what they do. The same principle applies when we become self-identified with the body or the intellect, but it is the emotions that are particularly critical for caregivers in an on-going crisis environment like that of working with the terminally ill.

Many of us end up interpreting Jesus' saying, "Come unto me all ye who are heavy laden, for my burden is light and my yoke is easy," as "Come unto *me*." Our tendency is to take on the burdens of others. And, although at first we may appear to be fed by the experience of getting our self-worth from giving to others, eventually we burnout. The burdens, the feelings of others, in turn become ours, and soon the burden becomes very heavy indeed. With our emotions attached, our own personal needs become involved in our work, our love ceases to be unconditional, and we are no longer a channel for the limitless resources of God's

Love. Our true effectiveness as servers has ended.

The inner centering, the drawing on that "well of living water," that results from the regular practice of identifying with and drawing on the qualities of our True Self for our sense of worth and identity is the single most effective preventative measure for burnout. We do not become numb or over-stimulated or detached, we are compassionate, but we are also reminded that compassion does not mean to feel the suffering of others and take it upon our self, but rather to feel *with* another. We are loving and unattached. Effective service, especially in the dying environment, depends on this. As caregivers we often need to learn, and be empowered, to take responsibility for our own care as well as others.

Achieving and maintaining this state of consciousness is not possible without the following of a spiritual discipline, and the development of such a spiritual practice is most readily facilitated when done in group formation through submitting oneself to a spiritual rule. When this personal practice is joined with a conscious participation in the shared spiritual rule of an intentional serving community, a group's power to effect creative change, carry healing love, and be an agent of transformation in the lives of their own members and of all they contact becomes very great indeed.

This understanding of the nature, invocation, and transmission of spiritual power is behind all the great monastic traditions and prayer communities of both East and West, as well as the healing foundation of "secular" groups like Alcoholics Anonymous. To be effective today, though, a spiritual rule must be adaptable to a very active life in the world, often involving working in a crisis environment, when a daily physical gathering of the group is impossible. It must as well be written in a language that is consonant with Christ's teachings, while at the same time not being a stumbling block for the non-Christian, as most serving and caregiver groups will be made up of individuals of mixed faith and belief systems.

This spiritual rule has been developed in response to this need. It outlines practical techniques and a realistic daily routine for the implementation of the basic spiritual laws.

Working behind the scenes yet very active over a long period of time as the spiritual director to serving groups of Christians, Buddhists, and other faiths, and himself a disciple of Christ, the world teacher known as D.K. has stated the basic requirements to be a member of a serving group in the following words. They form the basis of the spiritual rule and are worth memorizing:

To become a member of a serving group the rules are simple, and are three in number.

First, learn to practice harmlessness;

Then desire nothing for the separated self,

And thirdly, look for the sign of divinity in all.

First Rule

The rule states: "First, learn to practice harmlessness." How we function in a group with others is determined largely by our own inner relationship with ourself and the intention we set there. Harmlessness is an attitude or a state of mind, set consciously by our will, much like a filter, to which we then submit all our experience. When we set this intention, anything that is not in accord with harmlessness simply will not be allowed through into action. It is acknowledged and recognized, but filtered out. This conscious choice to submit oneself to an inner discipline is where we all start. D.K. has the following to say on the subject:

"Harmlessness is the expression of the life of the person who realizes themself to be everywhere, who lives consciously as a soul, whose nature is love, whose method is inclusiveness, and to whom all forms are alike in that they are but externalizations of the one infinite Being.

"Harmlessness springs from true understanding and control of the personality by the soul, which leads inevitably to spiritual expression in everyday life.

"It is a state of mind which in no way negates firm or even drastic action; it concerns motive and involves the determination that the motive behind all activity is goodwill.

"Let harmlessness therefore be the keynote of your life.

"An evening review should be carried forward entirely along this line. Divide the review work in three parts and consider:

1. Harmlessness in thought. This will primarily result in control of speech.

2. Harmlessness in emotional reaction. This will result in being a channel for the love aspect of the soul.

3. Harmlessness in act. This will produce poise, skill in action, and the release of the creative will.

"These three approaches should be practiced, noting their effect on one's own self and development, and their effect on all those we come in contact with.

"If harmlessness is the keynote of your life, you will do more to produce right harmonious conditions in your personality than any amount of discipline along other lines."

Second Rule

The second rule to become a member of a serving group states: "Desire nothing for the separated self". The separated self is the part of our being that imagines itself to be separate from others. It is often designated as the ego, and for many, especially in the early stages of discipleship, it constitutes the personal self with its own desires, needs, and wants. These needs are frequently separative, and do not take into consideration the good of others, the whole of ourselves, or the larger group purpose. When we desire for the separated self we create barriers between ourselves and others. Oppositions arise (my needs vs. your needs, us and them thinking, the enemy, civil war, etc.), and the ability to be a serving person or group is lost. This does not mean that we should ignore our needs, but rather that we should not place them between ourselves and others. We must continually shift our consciousness and change our attitude from "us-them" to "we." From looking for and affirming separation, to looking for and affirming commonality of serving purpose.

The tool to achieve this is the daily Disidentification Meditation. *(Given later in this chapter. -ed.)* This is also a preventative measure for burnout, as well as a way to develop and strengthen the consciousness of the True Self. This is accomplished over a period of time through the discipline of regular meditative practice. The True Self is by its very nature inclusive and group-conscious, both towards the parts of its own being and towards others. So, developing identification with our True Self, by disidentifying from the other parts of our being and *subordinating* them to our True Self, is a key practice. The other parts of our being are then brought into alignment and under the guidance and direction of the True Self.

Third Rule

The third rule states: "Look for the sign of divinity in all". Service has been defined as approaching every human being as a soul. This means to recognize that every living being is a child of God, has a spark of the divine in them, a reason for being and a loved place in God's plan, regardless of how disconnected from it they may be or what personality traits they may be manifesting, or what suffering may be present in their lives. This means, practically speaking, to always look for and see the good in others, and feed that. It does not mean being *unaware* of the not good or the destructive or the not likeable, but simply not to focus on, nor feed, those aspects of the person or the interaction.

When in a personal or group situation where this becomes a real challenge, the following affirmation has proven most helpful:

"I tread the lighted Way into the hearts of all. I serve my brother and my sister and their need. Those whom I, the little self, love not, I serve with joy because I love to serve."

When we take this attitude systematically towards ourselves and others, gradually that which is destructive or not life-affirming will be starved out and the other aspects of the self or interaction will grow. This approach of seeing the good and feeding it in all situations and people has been proven the most effective for creative growth and harmonious working relationships. To look for the sign of divinity in all is thus the application of spiritual law.

The Three Rules and Spiritual Law

All three of the rules are based on spiritual law. They have just as powerful spiritual effects as the physical laws have physical consequences. Just as with gravity, when we ignore them we fall! What happens in psychological terms is that when we consciously or unconsciously practice harmfulness, give in to desires of the separated self, or focus on the limitations in self or others, *that* becomes our identification and we are defined by those qualities. They become the controlling factors in our lives.

These three rules function as the deeply-considered practical application of spiritual law and are an extension of the universal law of love which we know in the form of the two great commandments: "Love God with all your heart and soul and strength and mind. And love your neighbor as yourself."

Daily Discipline

Morning Meditation/Prayer

We start the day by affirming who we really are, identifying consciously with our True Self, and setting by an act of will our intention for the day, choosing what attitude as well as what clothes to wear. And we give thanks, for nothing so maintains the health of our hearts as gratitude.

Use one of the meditations given in the following pages. About half an hour should be set aside daily for this, including some time to read sacred scripture, or any text which has a special, uplifting message for us.

The Noon Recollection

Take just a moment to step back from what you are doing and remember who you are, to realign with your True Self. You can do this wherever you are, no matter what you are doing. You may wish to repeat to yourself a phrase from your morning meditation such as "I am the Self;" or "I am the center of loving awareness;" or "I am a soul in joyful service;" or whatever works for you.

The Five O'Clock Prayer

Take a moment at five o'clock to again recollect who you are. Then be aware of your relatedness to all other serving souls, knowing that whatever our outer circumstances, none of us work alone. We all have our part in a greater loving purpose.

Know that at this time people all over the world are joining with you and that together we form a group of world servers.

Be particularly aware of those in any serving group you may be aligned with, and take a moment to make mental loving contact with them, knowing yourself to be supporting and supported by them. And give thanks.

The Evening Review

Take five or ten minutes at the end of the day before going to sleep to review (not relive), briefly, the events of the day. Take note of the thoughts, feelings, acts, and words which were part of your day, doing so with compassionate detachment, tolerance, and humor. To evoke these qualities of a loving witness, re-connect and identify again with the Self. Reinforce the connection with your sense of your own relationship with a loving personal God who is there to help you go back through the day to the moment of rising.

The review based on harmlessness may equally well be used. The main thing is to just see your day the way it was, release or forgive anything that needs to be released or forgiven for yourself or others, give thanks, and close the books.

As a caregiver, pay particular attention to any feeling states or thought forms you may have picked up from those you worked with in the course of the day, and then ask your self, "Is this mine?" If it is not, let it go.

If it stays with you, ask what part of yourself has been touched or hooked in. This awareness is part of your evening review.

If it has been a particularly stressful or difficult day, you may wish to take a shower, and while standing under the shower, imagine it is a shower of light that is streaming down upon you, cleansing you and washing down into the drain all the psychic accumulations of the day.

When you step out of the shower, before you dry, take a moment to shake the water from you, feeling your freedom and cleanness. Then imagine you are breathing in through the bottom of your feet, receiving energy from the earth, like a tree drawing nurture up through its roots. Done regularly, this practice will renew the body and prevent the taking on of the experiences of others.

The total daily discipline should take about forty-five minutes.

Disidentification Meditation in Outline Form

I have a body, but I am not my body.

Take a minute to be aware of the life and state of your body and to honor it. Listen to it, hear what it has to say, and be receptive to your body needs. And then recollect that the body is your instrument. It is not your Self.

I have a body, but it is not my Self. Pause and realize the truth of this.

I have emotions, but I am not my emotions.

Be aware of the life and state of your feelings and honor them. Listen to them, hear what they have to say, and be receptive to your emotional needs. And then recollect that your feelings too are your instrument. They are not your Self.

I have emotions, but they are not myself. Pause and realize the truth of this.

I have an intellect, but I am not my intellect.

Be aware now of your state of mind and your thought life and honor them. Listen to them, hear what they have to say, and be receptive to your mental needs. And then recollect that your mind too is your instrument. It is not your Self.

I have an intellect, but it is not myself. Pause and realize the truth of this.

Who am I then?

Move now beyond the contents of your consciousness into the One who is there, the perceiver, the *I am*.

I am the Self. The Self am I.

I am a center of pure *Self*consciousness, and of calm and vital awareness.

I am a center of *effortless will*, mastering, integrating, directing, and using as a field of service every aspect of my being.

More radiant than the Sun, purer than the snow, subtler than the ether, is the Self, the spirit within us. We are that Self, that Self are we.

Enter now into the consciousness of your True Self. You may wish to focus on a particular quality (unconditional love, joy, wisdom, peace, acceptance, etc.), or an appropriate *seed thought*, such as a line of scripture, or just be in silence. Spend a period of time here.

Close by saying your name silently to yourself to anchor this experience. Be again aware of the life of your mind, body, and emotions, but now in this aligned perspective, as an instrument of service, expression, and realization for your soul's purpose.

With practice, the disidentification phase of the meditation can proceed faster and greater emphasis and time can be placed in identifying with the True Self and experiencing and anchoring its nature and qualities.

Some people have found it helpful to tape this meditation. Rather than memorizing it, the important thing is to go through each of the stages taking as much time as is needed, ending with a period of Self-identification.

This meditation is an excellent way to start the day. You may wish to follow it with some scripture or study time. It is most effective when done daily for a minimum of three months so the inner process can begin to become reflexive. About ten to fifteen minutes should be given to the meditation, and then fifteen to twenty for the morning study (enough time to absorb one thought, one aspect of love in service in the world).

Disidentification Meditation— Long Form

Adapted from Roberto Assagioli.

I have a body, but I am not my body.

My body may be in different conditions of health or sickness; it may be rested or tired, but it is not my real "I." My body is my precious instrument of experience and action, but it is only an instrument. I honor my body. I will to treat it well, but it is not my *self*. *I have a body but I am not my body*. Pause and realize the truth of this.

I have emotions, but I am not my emotions.

They are countless, changing, contradictory, with alternations of attraction and repulsion, like and dislike, light and dark. And yet I know that I always remain I, my-self, in times of hope or despair, in happiness or unhappiness, in a state of irritation or calm. Since I can observe, understand, and discriminate my emotions, and then increasingly master, direct, and utilize them, it is evident that they are not my self. My emotions are my precious instrument of communication and aspiration. I honor my emotional life and will to maintain it in harmony and balance, but it is not myself. *I have emotions, but I am not my emotions.* Pause and realize the truth of this.

I have an intellect, but I am not my intellect.

It is more or less developed and active; undisciplined perhaps, but teachable. It is my precious instrument of knowledge in regard to the outer world as well as the inner, but it is not myself. I honor my intellect, and will to maintain it in harmony and balance and right relationship with all of my being. *I have an intellect, but I am not my intellect.* Pause and realize the truth of this.

Who am I then?

What remains after having disidentified myself from my body, my sensations, my feelings, my desires, my mind, my actions? It is the essence of myself—a center of pure *Self*consciousness. It is the permanent factor in the ever varying flow of my personal life. It is that which gives me a sense of beingness and from where I serve. I affirm my identity with this center and realize its permanence and energy. It is my *true self*.

I am the Self. I am a center of pure *Self*consciousness. I am a center of calm, vital awareness, and wise love. I am a center of *will*, mastering, directing, integrating, and using as a field of service every aspect of my being. *I am* the constant and unchanging SELF.

Spend a few minutes simply being in this place of the *true self*. You may wish to focus on particular qualities of the Self, such as unconditional love, joy, peace, etc., or contemplate these lines:

> *More radiant than the Sun, purer than the snow,*
> *subtler than the ether, is the Self, the spirit within us.*
> *We are that Self, that Self are we.*

To close, say your name to yourself three times, and as you do so, anchor the qualities of the *true self* in your personal life. Be again aware of your mind, body, and emotions, but now in this aligned perspective, as an instrument of service.

Identification Meditation

Adapted from Roberto Assagioli

I am the Self. The Self am I.
I am a center of pure self consciousness.
I am a center of calm, vital energy.

Take a moment now to look at the life of your body, emotions/feelings, mind/thoughts, and various subpersonalities. See them all as within your Self, as if the characters in a book that you, the Self, are writing.

I have will and can make choices. I can initiate action.

I can be in charge of my life. I will to be in charge of my life.

I have a physical body which is my precious instrument of experience and action. I will to nurture it and keep it well.

I have an emotional body and feelings which bring pleasure and displeasure. The choices I make, to a great extent, determine if I suffer or rejoice. My emotional body is my precious instrument of communication and aspiration. I will to maintain it in harmony and to nourish it well.

I have a mental body and an intellect I can use to reason, think, analyze, and plan. It is my precious instrument of perception and awareness in the outer world and in the inner world. I will to develop and train it well.

I have sub-personalities, but *I* am not my sub-personalities. I continually become more aware of them and the place of each one in my life. Each one has at its core the need to belong, the need to love and be loved, the need to creatively serve. Pause and realize the truth of this.

I will to be in charge of them. I will to meet my basic needs.

I will to be in charge of my life.

I am the Self. The Self am I.

More radiant than the Sun, purer than the snow, subtler than the ether, is the Self, the spirit within us.

We are that Self, that Self are we.

(Rest in the Self.)

Say your name silently to yourself three times. See the qualities of the Self and this experience manifesting in your personal life.

Healing Group Meditation

Take a moment to make yourself comfortable. Then close your eyes and be aware of your own breath, remembering that breath is spirit.

Following the Breath

On the in-breath, visualize that you are drawing the breath from the earth below, up through the bottom of the feet, and up the back to the top of the head; and on the out-breath that you are drawing the breath from the sky above down the front of your body and out your feet into the ground again. Follow the breath around for a few times and know that it is through our own being that we connect heaven and earth.

Contacting the Higher Self

Take a moment now to get in touch with your Higher Self or soul. It is the all-wise place of inner knowing in you, the quiet place of truth that loves all of you unconditionally, no matter how you or others may feel about you. It is the part of you that was there before you were born, chose every aspect of your being to work through in this lifetime, and will continue after your death. If you have never experienced this quality of being, just imagine that it is there, and in time the experience will come to fill the space you create for it. To help visualize it, you might think of it as a point of light about a foot and a half above your head. Now see that point of light as coming down and making contact with the center of the top of your head. As the connection is made, just feel the light going back and forth, and as it does so the center on the top of your head opens like a white flower to receive it, for this is where the spirit is said to traditionally enter into us.

Downpour/Cleansing

And now that point of light expands into a sun above you and pours its light down through your whole being, just as if you are standing in a shower of light. Allow this light to just wash down through you, washing back down into the ground anything that is standing in the way of your being here now, just as if you are standing in a shower of light.

Opening the Heart

God is love. To open ourselves to receive this love, we need first of all to open our own hearts. If it is appropriate for the group, recall that Jesus has promised us that whenever two or three are gathered together in his name, he himself will be there among us. Realize that his name is and always has been the name of love. And to open ourselves to love we need first of all to open our own hearts. The way in which we open our hearts is to know and experience ourselves as actively loving beings. So take a moment now to think of those people in your life whom you love and have loved. It does not matter if they are alive or dead, if the love was returned or not, or even if it is a love for a pet or a piece of music or a beautiful sunset, but simply that you love and have loved. Now allow that love to flow out of your heart to all those times and places and people. (And as you do so, you may feel a warmth in the center of your chest and may visualize the heart opening like a rose.)

Opening the Group Heart

Now allow this love to flow out of your heart to the one on the right. And as it goes around the group and comes back to you, just breathe it in, receiving even as you have given. Now breathe it out to the one on your left, and again as it comes back to you, just breathe it in and take your fill. And be aware now of the quality of this love, this living substance connecting all of us even though we are not touching, and be aware of how we have become one heart. Just like a tuning fork resonating to its own note, the love of God responds to its own note in us, entering into the group heart. Take a moment now to experience this resonance between your heart and the group heart and this coming in of greater Love. And as we breathe in and out, let us visualize that we are breathing this Love of God into our Group Heart. We are breathing in our fill, remembering that breath is spirit, and on our out-breath, we are breathing back out to God in thanksgiving. Take a minute now to follow this cycle of the breath of Love back and forth a few times between our Group Heart and God. For this is the first and great commandment, that we love the Lord our God with all our heart. As we continue, gradually be aware that the group heart is expanding, until its center is at the level of our hearts and the entire group is enclosed in it.

Loving Our Neighbor as Ourselves

The second great commandment is to love our neighbor as ourselves. So let us reach out now to join our hands with the ones next to us. As we do so, take a moment to feel the real physical contact and connection, for we are making the Word flesh. And now just allow that Love to flow out from your hearts and hands into the group. As it passes through you, breathe in your fill, breathe it into every cell of your being. Let it seek its own level in you, let it go wherever there is need of healing, for only Love heals and this is healing Love. And then let it overflow from you into the group. Gradually you may become aware that we have become a river of light, we have become one heart, one breath with God. We have become the heart of God.

Applying the Power of the Group

Take a moment now to visualize those individuals you may be aware of who are in need of this healing love. See them in the center of this group at the level of our heart, and as the heart of God breathe this love out to them and see them receiving it.

Now be aware of community and world situations where there is need of healing, and see them at the center of this group, and as one heart, breathe this love out to all those places.

Be aware that at the center of this group there is enough room and enough love for the whole world. And now let us visualize the Earth herself who is also in need of healing, at the center of this group. And as one, let love go out of us to this great living being in whom we live and move and have our being.

Closing

You may now drop hands again. Centered again in your own hearts, take a moment to feel the shift, how we are each separate individuals, and we also all are one. Feel a deep gratitude for this connectedness to Life, for being able to love and be loved and serve in this way. Now be aware of your feet planted firmly on the ground, rooted in the earth like a tree. Be aware of the sounds outside and the chair you are sitting in. Taking your time, when you are ready you may open your eyes.

Some Variations

A good way to end the group is for everyone to say together, "SO LET IT BE, AND HELP US TO DO OUR PART." If part of a religious service, this may effectively be followed by a loving dismissal such as "Go in peace to love and serve the Lord. Thanks be to God."

If the group is working with a particular theme, after opening the group heart, the group may then be asked on their next out-breath to raise their focus to a point between the eyebrows, and on their in-breath to breathe themselves into that center of the integrated personality, and then to spend a period of time contemplating some aspect of the study theme or a seed thought or a line of scripture. If the work to be done involves some personal processing, have them rise up through the open crown center to their Higher Self, rest in that space and feel its qualities for a time (unconditional love, peace, joy, knowing truth, etc.), and then do the work from that soul vantage point. At the end in either case, they can breathe themselves back down into the heart, and then proceed if desired to the loving our neighbor as ourself step.

Depending on time factors and the nature and focus of the group, Contacting the Higher Self and Downpour may be omitted, and of course the words may be shortened or otherwise adapted throughout. The important thing is the focus on the opening of the heart and the development of a serving group consciousness.

Home in Spirit

The following meditation by Dr. Edith Stauffer is quoted with permission from her book Unconditional Love and Forgiveness.

"Relax the body by breathing deeply or quietly, completely filling and slowly emptying the lungs. Be conscious and aware that life is breathing you. (You can alter your breath, but you cannot stop breathing.) Pause.

"Feel deep gratitude that life is flowing through you and causing your heart to beat. Feel yourself a part of that great life force, and feel gratitude for it. Pause.

"Feel love for the Source of life for designing such a beautiful life for you.

"Now imagine your Soul as a great light, like the sun, above your head. Pause. Imagine a beam of light flowing down into your mind and body. Pause. In your consciousness, move up that beam of light, above the Soul, into the home in spirit, that center of a feeling of calm energy. Pause. Experience a deep peace and rest. Pause. Let that spirit which is sound, wholesome, happy, and desirable fill your consciousness. Pause. Let it fill your mind and rest there—be at home in that spirit of rest and peace. Pause.

"Be at rest, allowing this spirit of peace to fill you, healing you and restoring you to perfect balance. Pause. See and feel your body healed and healthy, strong and vital. Let yourself rest in your home in spirit. Pause. Allow this energy of spirit which surrounds you to cleanse and heal all your emotions and feelings. Just accept this. Pause.

"Allow this mental rest and peace to fill your mind and heal it of all concerns. Rest here awhile (stay conscious). Feel the rest and peace. Pause.

"Now feel the energy, the essence of spirit flowing through your whole being, giving you peace and security. Pause.

"Be aware of the energy, the feeling of rest and well-being. Allow yourself to stay here for a few moments, feeling deep gratitude for the rest. Pause.

"Be willing now to let this force of spirit flow through you and out to all your relationships. Pause. Direct this feeling of well-being to your family, friends, and fellow beings. Radiate out, as beams of light, this feeling of wholeness. Pause. By an act of will, send out this spirit of home in spirit and release any strain in any of your relationships. See all your relationships as positive. Pause. Imagine all tensions being dissolved. See everyone as joyous. Pause. Now send out beams of light to all humanity. Pause.

"Now be aware of the beam of light flowing down to your own personality, the mental, emotional, and physical body. Pause. Now move down that beam of light and become aware of your physical body. Pause. Become aware of your breathing. Become aware of the room where you are and how you are sitting. Now open your eyes and look at your surroundings.

"You are now ready to continue with your activities, at the same time holding a subjective attitude which will bring back the feelings of rest and well-being.

"You may, if you wish, tape this exercise and listen to it as often as you wish. Should you become over-stimulated by using the tape or doing the exercise, discontinue it for a day or two. I highly recommend this exercise if you feel upset, burdened by concerns, or if you just need to rest."

Life-Transition Ministry

The purpose of life-transition ministry is to assist individuals in the transition out of physical life into non-physical life. It is offered to those who have requested assistance in making this transition as consciously as possible. It comes into play in addition to the other necessary medical, social, and psychological skills used in counseling and working with the dying. These works are all readily available, as are the details of the rites and sacraments of the individual faiths, so I will not attempt to duplicate them here.

The life-transition ministry focuses very narrowly on the period preceding physical death, during the letting go process, and after the release of the body. The specific tools used are the consciousness of the caregiver and the serving group, meditative prayer and directed energy, and a modified form of the disidentification meditation.

In this context the meditation requires the caregiver to lead it and the groundwork has to be laid for it, much like the psychological preparation for Last Rites. It is then presented with a very definite focus on soul identification and the qualities and experience of the soul as an independent being-ness, that has entered into incarnation working through a personal self and its vehicles of expression (body, mind, emotions), for a particular serving purpose and/or learning experience. The Soul is now returning to its source, with the growth of this lifetime, like an additional ring in the trunk of a tree, to continue its life on non-physical planes.

A good half an hour should be allowed for the meditation.

Meditation to Assist Life-Transition

Note: As the caregiver reads aloud the following, the dying person may respond, if able to do so, by repeating the litany of the disidentification meditation.

Are you ready to release the life of your body?

I have a body, but I am not my body.

Recollect and give thanks for the life of your body and its many states and aspects of expression in the course of your life, having served as a more or less adequate physical instrument for the expression of your soul purpose on earth. Be aware of the miracle of its myriad component parts, atoms, genes, cells, nerves, organs, muscles, blood and bone and water, etc., all working together for this period of time as an instrument of expression for you, the Self, a living soul, and now preparing to dissolve into the elements again and return to the common pool of undifferentiated matter from which spirit draws to create a living form on earth. Feel wonder for this process of dissolution as well as conception and creation, being especially grateful for the times when you have known, given, and received love through the body, through touch and physical affection, and then release your body with love and blessing and gratitude.

I have a body, but it is not my Self.

Take time to experience this, and when you are ready for the next step, raise your hand.

Are you ready now to release all identification with emotional life?

I have emotions, but I am not my emotions.

Recollect and give thanks for the life of your emotions and its many, many varying states and aspects of expression. Be aware of the countless feelings you have felt in your lifetime and expressed or not expressed, how they have served you and others well or not so well in different situations, what you gave to others, what you received from others, being especially grateful for those times when you have loved through the emotions and truly felt the love of others; and then release your emotional body with love and blessing and gratitude.

I have emotions, but they are not my Self.

Take time to experience this, and when you are ready for the next step, raise your hand.

Are you ready now to release all identification with mental life?

I have an intellect, but I am not my intellect.

Recollect and give thanks for the life of your mind and its growth over your lifetime, the more or less developed and disciplined state of it, its more or less effective use as an instrument to examine the inner world as well as the outer. Be aware of the myriad different thoughts, concepts, ideas that have passed through it, been expressed, taken in, the thoughtforms created and shared for good and for ill. Be especially grateful for the times when your mind and your thoughts have been an expression of inclusive love, opening doors, bringing understanding and awakening to others, and for those people and ideas that have brought that to you, and then release your mental body with love and blessing and thanksgiving.

I have an intellect, but it is not my Self.

Take time to experience this, and when you are ready for the next step, raise your hand.

Move now in consciousness into the one who IS.

> I am the Self, I am a living soul.
> I am a center of radiant life, and peace and joy.
> I am a center of wise, loving, silent will.

I am shifting my focus from expression on earth to the plane of my own being and to the eternal life of spirit.

I am drawing back into myself the fruits gained through my experience of embodied life, with deep and loving gratitude for my personal self. I know that you (say name) are not perfect, but that is not a requirement I ever had of you. I forgive and have forgiven you, for you are my disciple, a learner. I have chosen you of all possible human creation to be my reflection on earth, to grow through and to learn through and to love through. My love for you is unconditional, for I love as God loves.

Be aware of any acts or experiences for which the personal self is seeking forgiveness.

I now send my unconditional love and forgiveness, my acceptance and understanding, down to you, my personal self, my embodiment on earth and upon all aspects of the life you have lived, and I let you go in peace.

Allow your focus now to be only on the plane of soul, taking your time to accustom yourself like adjusting your eyes upon entering a very differently lighted room, and be aware of what is there, the quality and nature of this environment.

You may be aware of others who are no longer in the body, lovers, a spouse, parents and grandparents who have gone before, perhaps children, perhaps ancient friends, perhaps angels, those beings whose bodies are made of light instead of matter. They are there to assist you in the next stage of the transition out of physical life. They are there to assist you with the awarenesses, cleansing processes, and growth that go with the transition. Take a moment to be there.

Now let even all of this go, and just be at home in the spirit.

More radiant than the Sun, purer than the snow, subtler than the ether, am I.

I am a point of Light within a greater Light.
I am a strand of loving Energy within the stream of Love divine.
I am a point of sacrificial Fire, focused within the fiery Will of God.

I am that *I am*.

You may stay here as long as you wish. When you are ready, take on again whatever aspects of the outer garment you wish. Take on whichever mental, emotional, and physical expressions that are necessary and appropriate for you at this time.

As you re-enter your personal self do so with a deep and peaceful confidence in what has been, what is, and what is to be, for there is only life and you are now free; and give thanks for this re-affirmation of connection with the Source of life and for the unconditional love and forgiveness that you have received.

Assisting Individuals who are Unconscious or Cut-off from their Higher Self

If the individual you are working with is not conscious or because of belief systems or emotional state or attachments is not open to contact with their Higher Self or God, you can still be of direct assistance to the soul in the transition process, through, as appropriate, silent or spoken prayer.

Make contact and align yourself with your own soul, then consciously invoke the presence of Christ, Lord God, the blessed mother, or an appropriate saint or spiritual or angelic being, and pray that their love and wisdom guide you in assisting this individual. Then make contact with the soul of the one you are praying for and direct the energy of these living ones towards the person in transition. If you are aware of loved ones or relatives who have passed before you may wish to invoke their assistance as well. See the release as being accomplished and whatever degree of conscious soul-connection that is possible or appropriate being made with the personal self. If the life focus of the individual leaves no room for this experience, there may be a healing dream instead.

Here is an example of a dream a woman who had been very frightened of dying had on the day of her death:

> She sees a candle lit on the window sill of the hospital room and finds that the candle suddenly goes out. Fear and anxiety ensue as the darkness envelops her. Suddenly, the candle lights on the other side of the window and she awakens.
>
> From *On Dreams and Death*,
> by Marie Louise Von-Franz

The Inner Aspect of the Death Process

The actual death process is essentially the soul breaking loose of its vehicle of expression. This involves a kind of rhythmic pulling back and forth, like a boat casting off its mooring lines. Gradually, the directed energy of the soul becomes increasingly stronger until it has pulled loose the lifeness of the person and absorbed it back into itself, and all the many points of attachment it has formed to its mental, emotional, and physical body and through which its living energy flows down in to the personal self have been severed or pulled free. The Bible speaks of the "silver cord." It can also be seen as a radiant web, made up of filaments of light. Sometimes the souls release very readily and smoothly, or, as in cases of sudden death, they may break loose with a shock and all at once, or sometimes it may be a long and protracted process, drawn out with great struggle. These are the inner processes which accompany the outer clinical symptoms.

Remember at all times that the person's own soul or Higher Self is the true judge of where the individual is and what they need, *not* our own biases or theology. So always direct healing or other assisting energy directly to the soul to make use of as the soul sees fit, or release the individual directly to Christ or to the Blessed Mother. The same applies for praying and meditating upon individuals after they have passed.

Assisting Individuals after They Have Left the Body

It is often a good idea to tune in with the individual from time to time in the days following their leaving the body to make sure that they are free and clear or that someone has come to assist them. Since "energy follows thought," this is done by making contact and aligning oneself with one's own soul and then imagining (image-ing) the connection with the departed soul and receiving what comes in or is seen with inner vision. Sometimes in the hours or days after death, the individual may be quite confused or lost. If the struggle was very great, a lot of cleansing from the life lived may be needed, as the body may have been released, but emotional and mental attachments are still holding on. Again, always work only from love and directly soul to soul through the Christ or God as the apex of a visualized triangle of spiritual energy. Also, relatives or other loved ones may appear or be invoked to lead the disoriented one towards the light.

This "tuning in" is easier initially to just *do*, and then concern oneself later on with explaining and understanding, because most of us have been trained to rule out or not recognize the capacity for this perception, though in fact we all have it built into us. With regular practice, the facility and ability to make finer discriminations will steadily increase.

The traditional Christian prayers said at the time of death and afterwards for the departed ("Depart O Christian soul out of this world," and "Into your hands, O merciful Saviour we commend your servant," etc.), also assist life-transition.

This Rule and related material began as a response to human need. As a Resource, it is intended to continue to grow and be shaped by the experiences of those using and living with it. It will be most helpful if you share what works for you, your group, and the people you work with, what doesn't, and what adaptations have been called for as you apply these principles to your serving situation.

Opening the heart through the practice of the various steps of this Spiritual Rule for Caregivers can only increase the loving gifts we can offer to others as well as the gifts we give to ourselves.

The gift of transformation is an on-going process for each of us on our inner pathway.

The Living Will

TO MY FAMILY, PHYSICIAN, LAWYER,
   CLERGYMAN,
TO ANY MEDICAL FACILITY IN WHOSE CARE I
   HAPPEN TO BE,
TO ANY INDIVIDUAL WHO MAY BECOME
   RESPONSIBLE FOR MY HEALTH, WELFARE OR
   AFFAIRS,

Death is as much a reality as birth, growth, maturity and old age — it is one certainty of life. If the time comes when I, _____, can no longer take part in decisions for my own future, let this statement stand as an expression of my wishes, while I am still of sound mind.

If the situation should arise in which there is no reasonable expectation of my recovery from physical or mental disability, I request that I be allowed to die and not be kept alive by artificial means or "heroic measures." I do not fear death itself as much as the indignities of deterioration, dependence and hopeless pain. I therefore ask that medication be mercifully administered to me to alleviate suffering even though this may hasten the moment of death.

This request is made after careful consideration. I hope you who care for me will feel morally bound to follow its mandate. I recognize that this appears to place a heavy responsibility upon you, but it is with the intention of relieving you of such responsibility and placing it upon myself in accordance with my strong convictions, that this statement is made.

Signed _____

Date   _____

Witness _____

Witness _____

Copies of this request have been given to:

_____   _____

_____

DURABLE POWER OF ATTORNEY FOR HEALTH CARE©

(California Civil Code Sections 2410-2443)

This is a Durable Power of Attorney for Health Care form. By filling in this form, you can select someone to make health care decisions for you if for some reason you become unable to make those decisions for yourself. A properly completed form provides the best legal protection available to help ensure that your wishes will be respected.

READ THIS FORM CAREFULLY BEFORE FILLING IT OUT. EACH PARAGRAPH IN THE FORM CONTAINS INSTRUCTIONS. IT IS IMPORTANT THAT YOU FOLLOW THESE INSTRUCTIONS SO THAT YOUR WISHES MAY BE CARRIED OUT.

The following checklist is provided to help you fill out this form correctly. You may use this checklist to double check sections you may be unsure of as you fill in the form. You may also use this checklist to help make sure you have completed the form properly. If you have properly completed this form, you should be able to answer **yes** to each question in the checklist.

_____ 1. I am a California resident who is at least 18 years old, of sound mind and acting of my own free will.

_____ 2. The individuals I have selected as my agent and alternate agents to make health care decisions for me are are at least 18 years old and are *not*:

- my *treating* health care provider.

- an employee of my *treating* health care provider, unless the employee is related to me by blood, marriage or adoption.

- an operator of a community care facility (Community care facilities are sometimes called board and care homes. If you are unsure whether a person you are thinking of selecting operates a community care facility, you should ask that person.)

- an employee of a community care facility, unless the employee is related to me by blood, marriage or adoption.

_____ 3. I have talked with the individuals I have selected as my agent and alternate agents and these individuals have agreed to participate. (You may select someone who is not a California resident to act as your agent or alternate agent, but you should consider whether someone who lives far away will be available to make decisions for you if and when that may become necessary.)

_____ 4. I have read the instructions and completed paragraphs 4, 5, 6, 7, 8, and 9 to reflect my desires.

5. I have **signed** and **dated** the form.

6. I have either _____ had the form notarized; **or** _____ had the form properly witnessed:

_____ 1. I have obtained the signatures of two adult witnesses who personally know me.

_____ 2. Neither witness is:

 • my agent or alternate agent designated in this form.

 • a health care provider, or the employee of a health care provider.

 • a person who operates or is employed by a community care facility.

_____ 3. At least one witness is not related to me by blood, marriage, or adoption, and is not named in my will or so far as I know entitled to any part of my estate when I die.

_____ 7. I HAVE GIVEN A COPY OF THE COMPLETED FORM TO THOSE PEOPLE INCLUDING MY AGENT, ALTERNATE AGENTS, FAMILY MEMBERS AND DOCTOR, WHO MAY NEED THIS FORM IN CASE AN EMERGENCY REQUIRES A DECISION CONCERNING MY HEALTH CARE.

SPECIAL REQUIREMENTS

_____ 8. **Patients in Skilled Nursing Facilities.**

 If I am a patient in a skilled nursing facility, I have obtained the signature of a patient advocate or ombudsman. (If you are not sure whether you are in a skilled nursing facility, you should ask the people taking care of you.)

_____ 9. **Conservatees under the Lanterman-Petris-Short Act.**

 If I am a conservatee under the Lanterman-Petris-Short Act and want to select my conservator as my agent or alternate agent to make health care decisions, I have obtained a laywer's certification. (If you are not sure whether the person you wish to select as your agent is your conservator under the Lanterman-Petris-Short Act, you should ask that person.)

If you change your mind about who you would like to make health care decisions for you, or about any of the other statements you have made in this form, you should take all of the following steps: 1. Complete a new form with the changes you desire; 2. Tell everyone who got a copy of the old form that it is no longer valid and ask that copies of the old form be returned to you so you may destroy them; 3. Give copies of the new form to the people who may need the form to carry out your wishes as described above in number 7. If after reading this material you still have unanswered questions, you should talk to your doctor or a lawyer.

©California Medical Association 1986 (revised)

DURABLE POWER OF ATTORNEY
FOR HEALTH CARE DECISIONS

(California Civil Code Sections 2410-2443)

WARNING TO PERSON EXECUTING THIS DOCUMENT

This is an important legal document. Before executing this document, you should know these important facts:

This document gives the person you designate as your agent (the attorney-in-fact) the power to make health care decisions for you. Your agent must act consistently with your desires as stated in this document or otherwise made known.

Except as you otherwise specify in this document, this document gives your agent the power to consent to your doctor not giving treatment or stopping treatment necessary to keep you alive.

Notwithstanding this document, you have the right to make medical and other health care decisions for yourself so long as you can give informed consent with respect to the particular decision. In addition, no treatment may be given to you over your objection, and health care necessary to keep you alive may not be stopped or withheld if you object at the time.

This document gives your agent authority to consent, to refuse to consent, or to withdraw consent to any care, treatment, service, or procedure to maintain diagnose, or treat a physical or mental condition. This power is subject to any statement of your desires and any limitations that you include in this document. You may state in this document any types of treatment that you do not desire. In addition, a court can take away the power of your agent to make health care decisions for you if your agent (1) authorizes anything that is illegal, (2) acts contrary to your known desires or (3) where your desires are not known, does anything that is clearly contrary to your best interests.

Unless you specify a shorter period in this document, this power will exist for seven years from the date you execute this document and, if you are unable to make health care decisions for yourself at the time when this seven-year period ends, this power will continue to exist until the time when you become able to make health care decisions for yourself.

You have the right to revoke the authority of your agent by notifying your agent or your treating doctor, hospital, or other health care provider orally or in writing of the revocation.

Your agent has the right to examine your medical records and to consent to their disclosure unless you limit this right in this document.

Unless you otherwise specify in this document, this document gives your agent the power after you die to (1) authorize an autopsy, (2) donate your body or parts thereof for transplant or therapeutic or educational or scientific purposes, and (3) direct the disposition of your remains.

If there is anything in this document that you do not understand, you should ask a lawyer to explain it to you.

1. CREATION OF DURABLE POWER OF ATTORNEY FOR HEALTH CARE

By this document I intend to create a durable power of attorney by appointing the person designated above to make health care decisions for me as allowed by Sections 2410 to 2443, inclusive, of the California Civil Code. This power of attorney shall not be affected by my subsequent incapacity.

2. DESIGNATION OF HEALTH CARE AGENT

(Insert the name and address of the person you wish to designate as your agent to make health care decisions for you. None of the following may be designated as your agent: (1) your treating health care provider, (2) a nonrelative employee of your treating health care provider, (3) an operator of a community care facility, or (4) a nonrelative employee of an operator of a community care facility.)

I, _____
(insert your name)

do hereby designate and appoint: Name: _____

Address: _____

Telephone Number: _____ as my attorney-in-fact (agent)
to make health care decisions for me as authorized in this document.

3. GENERAL STATEMENT OF AUTHORITY GRANTED

If I become incapable of giving informed consent to health care decisions, I hereby grant to my agent full power and authority to make health care decisions for me including the right to consent, refuse consent, or withdraw consent to any care, treatment, service, or procedure to maintain, diagnose or treat a physical or mental condition, and to receive and to consent to the release of medical information, subject to the statement of desires, special provisions and limitations set out in paragraph 4.

4. STATEMENT OF DESIRES, SPECIAL PROVISIONS, AND LIMITATIONS

(Your agent must make health care decisions that are consistent with your known desires. You can, but are not required to, state your desires in the space provided below. You should consider whether you want to include a statement of your desires concerning decisions to withhold or remove life-sustaining treatment. For your convenience, some general statements concerning the withholding and removal of life-sustaining treatment are set out below. If you agree with one of these statements, you may INITIAL that statement. READ ALL OF THESE STATEMENTS CAREFULLY BEFORE YOU SELECT ONE TO INITIAL. You can also write your own statement concerning life-sustaining treatment and/or other matters relating to your health care. BY LAW, YOUR AGENT IS NOT PERMITTED TO CONSENT ON YOUR BEHALF TO ANY OF THE FOLLOWING: COMMITMENT TO OR PLACEMENT IN A MENTAL HEALTH TREATMENT FACILITY, CONVULSIVE TREATMENT, PSYCHOSURGERY, STERILIZATION OR ABORTION. In

every other respect, your agent may make health care decisions for you to the same extent you could make them for yourself if you were capable of doing so. If you want to limit in any other way the authority given your agent by this document, you should state the limits in the space below. If you do not initial one of the printed statements or write your own statement, your agent will have the broad powers to make health care decisions on your behalf which are set forth in Paragraph 3, except to the extent that there are limits provided by law.)

I do **not** want my life to be prolonged and I do **not** want life-sustaining treatment to be provided or continued if the burdens of the treatment outweigh the expected benefits. I want my agent to consider the relief of suffering and the quality as well as the extent of the possible extension of my life in making decisions concerning life-sustaining treatment.

I want my life to be prolonged and I want life-sustaining treatment to be provided **unless I am in a coma** which my doctors reasonably believe to be irreversible. Once my doctors have reasonably concluded I am in an irreversible coma, I do **not** want life-sustaining treatment to be provided or continued.

I want my life to be prolonged to the greatest extent possible without regard to my condition, the chances I have for recovery or the cost of the procedures.

If this statement reflects your desires, initial here _____.

If this statement reflects your desires, initial here _____.

If this statement reflects your desires, initial here _____.

Other or additional statements or desires, special provisions, or limitations.

_____

_____

(You may attach additional pages if you need more space to complete your statement. If you attach additional pages, you must DATE and SIGN EACH PAGE.)

3

5. CONTRIBUTION OF ANATOMICAL GIFT

(You may choose to make a gift of all or part of your body to a hospital, physician, or medical school for scientific, educational, therapeutic or transplant purposes. Such a gift is allowed by California's Uniform Anatomical Gift Act. If you do not make such a gift, you may authorize your agent to do so, or a member of your family may make a gift unless you give them notice that you do not want a gift made. In the space below you may make a gift yourself or state that you do not want to make a gift. If you do not complete this section, your agent will have the authority to make a gift of all or a part of your body under the Uniform Anatomical Gift Act.)

If either statement reflects your desires, sign on the line next to the statement. **You do not have to sign either statement.** If you do not sign either statement, your agent and your family will have the authority to make a gift of all or part of your body under the Uniform Anatomical Gift Act.

(_____)   Pursuant to the Uniform Anatomical Gift Act, I hereby give, effective upon my death:

  (signature)   ☐ Any needed organ or parts; or

                                 ☐ The parts or organs listed:

                                 _____

                                 _____

                                 _____

(_____)   I do not want to make a gift under the Uniform Anatomical Gift Act, nor do I want my agent or family to do so.

  (signature)

6. AUTOPSY AND DISPOSITION OF MY REMAINS

I understand that my agent will be able to authorize an autopsy (an examination of my body after my death to determine the cause of my death) and to direct the disposition of my remains unless I limit that authority in this document. I also understand that my agent or any other person who directs the disposition of my remains must follow any instructions I have given in a written contract for funeral services, my will or by some other method.

⌂

(OPTIONAL: If you do not want your agent to be involved in these matters, you should state your desires concerning an autopsy and the person you would like to direct the disposition of your remains. If any of the statements below reflect your desires, sign next to that statement. If none of these statements reflect your desires and you want to limit the authority of your agent to consent to an autopsy and/or to dispose of your remains, you should write your own statement in paragraph 4, above.)

Autopsy

(_____)
   (signature)

I hereby consent to an examination of my body after my death to determine the cause of my death.

(_____)
   (signature)

My agent may not authorize an autopsy.

Disposition of Remains

(_____)
   (signature)

My agent may not direct the disposition of my remains and I would prefer that _____
                            (name and address)

_____ direct the disposition of my remains.

(_____)
   (signature)

I have described the way I want my remains disposed of in (circle one):
1. A written contract for funeral services with

_____
         (name of mortuary/cemetery)

2. My will
3. Other:

7. DESIGNATION OF ALTERNATE AGENTS

(You are not required to designate any alternate agents but you may do so. Any alternative agent you designate will be able to make the same health care decisions as the agent designated in Paragraph 2, above, in the event that agent is unable or unwilling to act as your agent. Also, if the agent designated in Paragraph 2 is your spouse, his or her designation as your agent is automatically revoked by law if your marriage is dissolved.)

If the person designated in Paragraph 2 as my agent is not available and willing to make a health care decision for me, then I designate the following persons to serve as my agent to make health care decisions for me as authorized in this document, such persons to serve in the order listed below:

A. First Alternative Agent

Name: _____

Address: _____

Telephone Number: _____

B. Second Alternative Agent

Name: _____

Address: _____

Telephone Number: _____

8. DURATION

I understand that this power of attorney will exist for seven years from the date I execute this document unless I establish a shorter time. If I am unable to make health care decisions for myself when this power of attorney expires, the authority I have granted my agent will continue to exist until the time when I become able to make health care decisions for myself.

(Optional) I wish to have this power of attorney end before seven years on the following date: _____.
(Fill in this space ONLY if you want the authority of your agent to end EARLIER than the seven-year period described above.)

9. NOMINATION OF CONSERVATOR OF MY PERSON

(A conservator of the person may be appointed for you if a court decides that you are unable properly to provide for your personal needs for physical health, food, clothing or shelter. The appointment of a conservator may affect, or transfer to the conservator your right to control your physical care, including under some circumstances your right to make health care decisions. You are not required to nominate a conservator but you may do so. The court will appoint the person you nominate unless that would be contrary to your best interests. You may, but are not required to, nominate as your conservator the same person you named in paragraph 2 as your health care agent. You can nominate an individual as your conservator by completing the space below.)

If a conservator of the person is to be appointed for me, I nominate the following individual to serve as conservator of the person:

Name: _____

Address: _____

Telephone Number: _____

10. PRIOR DESIGNATIONS REVOKED

I revoke any prior durable power of attorney for health care.

Date and Signature of Principal

(YOU MUST DATE AND SIGN THIS POWER OF ATTORNEY)

I sign my name to this Durable Power of Attorney for Health Care on _____ at

(Date)

_____ , _____

(City)   *(State)*

_____

(Signature of Principal)

(THIS POWER OF ATTORNEY WILL NOT BE VALID FOR MAKING HEALTH CARE DECISIONS UNLESS IT IS EITHER: (1) SIGNED BY TWO QUALIFIED ADULT WITNESSES WHO ARE PERSONALLY KNOWN TO YOU AND WHO ARE PRESENT WHEN YOU SIGN OR ACKNOWLEDGE YOUR SIGNATURE OR (2) ACKNOWLEDGED BEFORE A NOTARY PUBLIC IN CALIFORNIA.)

CERTIFICATE OF ACKNOWLEDGEMENT OF NOTARY PUBLIC

(You may use acknowledgment before a notary public instead of the statement of witnesses which appears on the following page.)

State of California)
) ss.
County of _____)

On this _____ day of _____, in the year _____,

before me, _____
                        (here insert name of notary public)

personally appeared _____,
                              (here insert name of principal)

personally known to me (or proved to me on the basis of satisfactory evidence) to be the person whose name is subscribed to this instrument, and acknowledged that he or she executed it. I declare under penalty of perjury that the person whose name is subscribed to this instrument appears to be of sound mind and under no duress, fraud, or undue influence.

NOTARY SEAL

_____
(Signature of Notary Public)

6

STATEMENT OF WITNESSES

(If you elect to use witnesses instead of having this document notarized, you must use two qualified adult witnesses. None of the following may be used as a witness: (1) a person you designate as your agent or alternate agent, (2) a health care provider, (3) an employee of a health care provider, (4) the operator of a community care facility, (5) an employee of an operator of a community care facility. At least one of the witnesses must make the additional declaration set out following the place where the witnesses sign.)

I declare under penalty of perjury under the laws of California that the person who signed or acknowledged this document is personally known to me to be the principal, that the principal signed or acknowledged this durable power of attorney in my presence, that the principal appears to be of sound mind and under no duress, fraud, or undue influence, that I am not the person appointed as attorney-in-fact by this document, and that I am not a health care provider, an employee of a health care provider, the operator of a community care facility, nor an employee of an operator of a community care facility.

Signature: _____   Residence Address: _____

Print Name: _____

Date: _____

Signature: _____   Residence Address: _____

Print Name: _____

Date: _____

(AT LEAST ONE OF THE ABOVE WITNESSES MUST ALSO SIGN THE FOLLOWING DECLARATION.)

I further declare under penalty of perjury under the laws of California that I am not related to the principal by blood, marriage, or adoption, and, to the best of my knowledge I am not entitled to any part of the estate of the principal upon the death of the principal under a will now existing or by operation of law.

Signature: _____

(Optional Second Signature): _____

COPIES

YOUR AGENT MAY NEED THIS DOCUMENT IMMEDIATELY IN CASE OF AN EMERGENCY THAT REQUIRES A DECISION CONCERNING YOUR HEALTH CARE. YOU SHOULD KEEP THE EXECUTED ORIGINAL DOCUMENT AND GIVE A COPY OF THE EXECUTED ORIGINAL TO YOUR AGENT AND ANY ALTERNATE AGENTS. YOU SHOULD ALSO GIVE A COPY TO YOUR DOCTOR, MEMBERS OF YOUR FAMILY, AND ANY OTHER PEOPLE WHO WOULD BE LIKELY TO NEED A COPY OF THIS FORM TO CARRY OUT YOUR WISHES. PHOTOCOPIES OF THIS DOCUMENT CAN BE RELIED UPON AS THOUGH THEY WERE ORIGINALS.

SPECIAL REQUIREMENTS

(Special additional requirements must be satisfied for this document to be valid if (1) you are a patient in a skilled nursing facility or (2) you are a conservatee under the Lanterman-Petris-Short Act and you are appointing the conservator as your agent to make health care decisions for you. If you are not sure whether you are in a skilled nursing facility, which is a special type of nursing home, ask the facility staff. If you are not sure whether the person you want to choose as your health care agent is your conservator under the Lanterman-Petris-Short Act, ask that person.)

1. If you are a patient in a skilled nursing facility (as defined in Health and Safety Code Section 1250(c)) at least one of the witnesses must be a patient advocate or ombudsman. The patient advocate or ombudsman must sign the witness statement **and** must also sign the following declaration:

I further declare under penalty of perjury under the laws of California that I am a patient advocate or ombudsman as designated by the State Department of Aging and am serving as a witness as required by subdivision (f) of Civil Code 2432.

Signature: _____   Address: _____

Print Name:_____   _____

Date:_____   _____

2. If you are a conservatee under the Lanterman-Petris-Short Act (of Division 5 of the Welfare and Institutions Code) and you wish to designate your conservator as your agent to make health care decisions, you must be represented by legal counsel. Your lawyer must also sign the following statement:

I am a lawyer authorized to practice law in the state where this power of attorney was executed, and the principal was my client at the time this power of attorney was executed. I have advised my client concerning his or her rights in connection with this power of attorney and the applicable law and the consequences of signing or not signing this power of attorney, and my client, after being so advised, has executed this power of attorney.

Signature: _____   Address: _____

Print Name: _____   _____

Date: _____   _____

California Medical Association
P.O. Box 7690, San Francisco 94120-7690

Resource Guide

Organizations

AIDS Project Los Angeles
3670 Wilshire Blvd.,
Suite 300
Los Angeles, CA 90010
(213) 380-2000

California Medical
Association
44 Gough St.
P.O. Box 7690
San Francisco, CA 94120
(For information on the
Durable Power of Attorney
For Health Care)

Center For Attitudinal
Healing (Gerald Jampolsky)
21 Main Street
Tiburon, CA 94920
(415) 435-1622

Center For Help
In Time Of Loss
600 Blue Hill Rd.
River Vale, NJ 07675
(201) 391-4473

Chapel of St. John
Reverend John
Alexis-Viereck
1550 Mesmer
Culver City, CA
(213) 822-3643

Chelsea Psychotherapy
Associates
80 Eighth Ave., Suite 1305
New York, New York 10011
(212) 206-0045

Elisabeth Kubler-Ross
Center
S. Route 616
Headwaters, VA 24442
(703) 396-3441

Light of Christ Church
Reverend Carol
Parrish-Harra
Sparrow Hawk Village
P.O. Box 1274
Tahlequa, OK 74464

Los Angeles Center
For Living
1600 N. Sierra Bonita
Los Angeles, CA 90046
(213) 850-0877
(213) 850-0878

M.A.P.
(Mother of AIDS Patients)
P.O. Box 1763
Lomita, CA 90717
Barbara Cleaver
(213) 530-2109
(Information on The PWA
National AIDS Bracelet
Program may be obtained
from MAP)

Nechama - A Jewish Re-
sponse To AIDS
"Nechama means comfort"
6000 West Pico Blvd.
Los Angeles, CA 90035
(213) 934-2617

Progressive Nursing
Services
8235 Santa Monica Blvd.,
Suite 211
West Hollywood, CA 90046
(213) 650-1800

Psychosynthesis International
P.O. Box 926
Diamond Springs, CA 95619

Shanti Project
890 Hayes St.
San Francisco, CA 94117
(415) 558-9644

St. Augustine By-The-Sea
Reverend John
Alexis-Viereck
1227 4th St.
Santa Monica, CA 90401

United Spirit Church
Reverend Ron &
Sandy Scott
6671 Sunset Blvd, #1510
Hollywood, CA 90028
(213) 466-1900

Unity By-The-Sea
Reverend Margie
Ann Nicola
1245 4th St.
Santa Monica, CA 90401
(213) 393-0213

We have found the
following books and tapes
to be useful:

AIDS: A Self-Care Manual,
AIDS Project Los Angeles;
IBS Press, 1987.*

A Course In Miracles,
Foundation For Inner Peace

A Guidance Through Death
(audio tape)
Available from Cassandra
Christenson, through
The Los Angeles Center For
Living (213) 850-0877

Love Is Letting Go Of Fear,
Gerald Jampolsky; Bantam
Books, 1981.

*A New Age Handbook On
Death And Dying*, Carol
Parrish-Harra; IBS Press,
1988.*

*Stepping Stones To Grief
Recovery*, Deborah Roth;
IBS Press, 1988.*

*Unconditional Love And
Forgiveness*, Edith Stauffer;
Triangle publishers, 1987.

*When Someone You Love Has
AIDS: A Book of Hope for
Family and Friends*,
BettyClare Moffatt; NAL
Penguin, 1987.*

Marianne Williamson Audio
Tapes and Course
Information
Miracle Projects
7960 Selma, #305
Los Angeles, CA 90046
(213)650-3167

*These books may be
 ordered directly from
 IBS Press
 744 Pier Ave.
 Santa Monica, CA 90405
 (213) 450-6485